Texas
Politics
and
Government

TEXAS
POLITICS AND GOVERNMENT
A Concise Survey

Kim Quaile Hill and Kenneth R. Mladenka

TEXAS A&M UNIVERSITY

MACMILLAN PUBLISHING COMPANY
NEW YORK
Maxwell Macmillan Canada
TORONTO

Editor: Bruce Nichols
Production Supervisor: Ann-Marie WongSam
Production Manager: Muriel Underwood
Cover Designer: Robert Vega

This book was set in New Baskerville and Corvinus type by Americomp
and was printed and bound by R. R. Donnelley & Sons Company.
The cover was printed by New England Book Components.

Macmillan Publishing Company
866 Third Avenue, New York, New York 10022

Macmillan Publishing Company is part of
the Maxwell Communication Group of Companies.

Maxwell Macmillan Canada, Inc.
1200 Eglinton Avenue East
Suite 200
Don Mills, Ontario M3C 3N1

LIBRARY OF CONGRESS CATALOGING-IN-PUBLICATION DATA
Hill, Kim Quaile, 1946–
    Texas politics and government : a concise survey / Kim Quaile Hill
and Kenneth R. Mladenka.
        p. cm.
    Includes index.
    ISBN 0-02-354855-X (pbk.)
    1. Texas—Politics and government. 2. Local government—Texas.
    I. Mladenka, Kenneth R., 1943– . II. Title.
    JK4816.H55 1993
    320.4764–dc20   92-8330
                    CIP
Printing: 1 2 3 4 5 6 7   Year: 3 4 5 6 7 8 9

Preface

This book is intended to offer a brief, engaging survey of Texas state and local governments. The most important governmental institutions and political processes are discussed, and their most essential features are explained. Beyond those elemental matters, our intention has been to explore some key themes and concerns that illustrate why these governments are important and merit study.

We are concerned, first, with the extent to which these governments are democratic. Thus we raise that matter in a number of chapters, and we frequently observe how individual citizens can become involved in the governing process. We discuss, in particular, how one can participate in elections and have active involvement in political parties and interest groups. We also discuss some notable programs and services provided by Texas governments to illustrate activities that might especially stimulate the interest and involvement of citizens. This topic leads to the second concern of the book.

Our second concern is with the profound influences these governments have on the lives of Texans today. This is the case in good part because, as explained in Chapters 1 and 2, Texans have created "big government" and frequently demand even bigger government. State and local governments in Texas are already charged with a host of social and economic policy responsibilities, and we frequently demand even more responsibilities, services, and benefits from these governments. Such expectations are common and widespread among Texans in spite of the fact that most of us claim to prefer limited government with relatively few responsibilities.

Big governments will inevitably affect our lives in a variety of ways. Their success—or failure—at developing the economy, for example, will influence our personal economic opportunities. Similarly, their efforts in public education, environmental preservation, crime control, pollution control, and a host of other activities shape the quality of our everyday lives. We hope to receive important benefits from such governments, but we also yield to them considerable power to restrict our behavior. These few examples also illustrate how the second concern of this book is closely related to the first. If government influences our lives so intimately, we have particular reasons to be interested in the quality of the democratic process and to seek to shape government policies through direct participation. We have good reasons, that is, for wanting to stand up and be counted.

This book explores the character of Texas governments and the varied possibilities for participation in their decisions. By studying political party and interest group systems we learn the sources of some of the most important public demands for government action. By examining the institutions of state government (such as the legislature and the governor) and the separate levels of local government (such as cities, counties, and school districts), we can understand the particular responsibilities each institution and level of government assumes. We examine the courts and the legal system, too, to illustrate how individual Texans become involved in legal cases and how such cases are settled. We also examine in some detail the regulatory, subsidy, and social services responsibilities of these governments to see how they carry out these especially important functions.

Finally, we gratefully acknowledge here the assistance of several individuals who helped us produce this work. Our editor, Bruce Nichols, worked closely with us throughout the project to shape its character. Several reviewers of earlier versions of the manuscript also proved quite helpful. They include William M.

Pearson of Lamar University, Haywood T. Sanders of Trinity University, W. A. Hoffman of Del Mar College, James A. Puetz of North Harris County College, Tom Bass of the University of St. Thomas, and Robert D. Wrinkle of the University of Texas at Pan American. We took their advice on a number of points, but stubbornly refused to yield on several others. Whether the book is better or worse for our stubbornness must be left to the judgment of our readers.

K.Q.H.
K.R.M.

Contents

Texas
Politics
and
Government

1

Texans and Their Governments

". . . there are (places) where fable, myth, preconception, love, longing or prejudice step in and so distort a cool, clear appraisal that a kind of high-colored magical confusion takes permanent hold . . . surely Texas is such a place."

John Steinbeck

"There is something different and special about Texas and Texans."

T. R. Fehrenbach

Maybe we're prejudiced because we're Texans ourselves, but we also think there is something special about Texas. And that "something" makes Texas *government* special, too. Yet it is hard to say precisely what sets Texas apart from other states. We suspect that it is a combination of several unusual characteristics of the state, of the experiences of those who live here today, and of those who did so through its history. That combination of characteristics makes Texas unusual, but it also creates unusual problems for the governments of the state.

It's a Big State

Some of the state's characteristics are well known—at least in part. Take the most obvious—the state's size. Every American knows Texas is big. And every Texan probably suspects that if the polar ice cap ever melted, Alaska would shrink to no bigger than the second-largest state. But Texas is big in other ways than just its geographic size.

Texas has a big population, first. With approximately seventeen million residents, Texas is the third-largest state in the nation, behind California and New York and ahead of Florida, which ranks a distant fourth. Other comparisons indicate just how big the state is relative to other American states. Our population is about three and a half times as big as that of the average state, and it's about equal to the total population of the seventeen smallest states!

Texas is big by international standards, too. If Texas were a country in Western Europe, for example, its population would rank it the sixth-largest of twenty-one nations. If Texas were a continental Latin American nation, it would be the seventh-largest of twenty nations in that region. The Hispanic population of the state of Texas alone is as big as or bigger than the populations of nine of those Latin American nations.

Texas also has a big economy. The size of a state's economy is measured by its *gross state product,* the total monetary value of all the goods and services produced in the state in a given year. By this measure, Texas has the third-largest state economy in the United States, ranking after those of California and New York and well ahead of Illinois in fourth place. And Texas's gross state product is almost four times as large as that of the average state.

Our economy is big even by international standards. The economies of nations are compared with each other by way of their *gross national product,* which is the total monetary value of all goods and services produced in the nation in a year. Texas's gross state product, for example, is bigger than the gross national product of all but four of the nations of Western Europe.

In addition, and maybe as a surprise to many of our readers, Texas has a big government. Better put, Texas has big governments in the plural. The largest, of course, is the state government. The annual budget of the state government was $23.5 billion in 1991. If we equate a government's budget with a private corporation's total sales, Texas state government would be equivalent in size to companies ranked between 15 and 20 on the

Fortune 500 list of the largest American industrial corporations. The state government also employs about 250,000 people, more than any other employer in the state. Our biggest city governments are equally remarkable. The four largest cities in the state—Houston, Dallas, San Antonio, and Austin—all have annual budgets exceeding one billion dollars. And each of the four employs over ten thousand city workers. Local governments are, of course, created by and exist under the rules of the state government. And the combined budgets of Texas state and local governments in recent years have been as big as private corporations ranked between 5 and 10 on the *Fortune* 500 list.

And it's not just the size of our governments that is notable. Their number is impressive, too. There are in the state today 1,156 cities, 254 counties, 1,113 school districts, and 1,892 other special districts. Virtually all of these bodies are run by publicly elected officials who are supposed to carry out their functions the way average citizens desire. And all those governments can levy taxes on us and spend the resulting tax revenues, supposedly to make our lives better.

So what? Does size matter for more than bragging rights? We believe it certainly matters for state and local governments. Big, populous states with large economies are more difficult to govern. They encounter more public policy problems. Their economies are more diverse and require a broader range of government responsibilities and services. And big governments are themselves more difficult for the citizenry to control.

It's a Diverse State

Another characteristic that sets Texas apart is its diversity. Some of that is geographic, too. Geographers have identified eight major types of physical terrain that exist in the United States. Four of those types exist in Texas—the Gulf Coastal Plain, the Interior Lowlands, the Great Plains, and the Intermontane Plateaus. The overwhelming majority of states, on the other hand, exhibit only one or two types. Further, as Jordan, Bean, and Holmes (1984:7) observe, "Virtually all known weather phenomena frequent the state, resulting in climatic variation and vegetational striation unsurpassed by most other regions of comparable size in the world." This complexity of physical terrain, climate, soil, and vegetation means that opportunities for agriculture, mining, manufacturing, urban settlement, and outdoor activity—and for economic and social diversity generally—are remarkable.

Our population is a "melting pot" of diversity as well. The stereotypic Texan is an Anglo-Saxon whose family roots are in the Deep South of the United States. But successive waves of migration from other parts of the nation and the world have created a population that mirrors the patchwork quilt that the stereotypic Texan's ancestors might have brought on their journey to the state.

Consider as some examples of that patchwork the following facts: The 1990 U.S. census indicated that the Texas population is one of the nation's most diverse in its ethnic composition. About 26 percent of Texans are Hispanics. While the bulk of those Texans are of Mexican origin, there are also large numbers of Hispanics from several Latin, especially Central American, nations. About 12 percent of Texans are black and mostly longtime Texas natives. Yet a notable number of blacks are relatively recent immigrants from a variety of African nations. Finally, about 2 percent of Texans are Asian, including especially large numbers of Chinese, Vietnamese, Thais, and Koreans. Even our Anglo-Saxon population is quite a mix today. Former "Yankees," midwesterners, and westerners seem nearly as prevalent as "native Texans."

Different periods of migration to Texas also brought people with vastly different attitudes toward government, who experienced quite different problems once they arrived in the state. Consider just a couple of examples of those attitudes. The ancestors of the stereotypic Anglo-Saxon Texan we mentioned above migrated to the state in the 1800s from the Deep South. They were rugged individualists who did not expect government to do a great deal for them or for anyone else. And they passed those attitudes to their children and grandchildren.

Other migrants to the state, coming later, brought radically different ideas about government. Consider the sizable wave of "Sunbelt" migrants who came to Texas from the states of the Northeast, Midwest, and West in the 1970s and early 1980s. Most of these people were leaving states suffering bad economic times while Texas's economy was booming. They were attracted by the economic opportunities here, but they also came from states where rugged individualism was not the typical culture. They were often accustomed to government taking considerable responsibility for social and economic problems because that's what citizens demanded.

We could describe several other distinctive sets of Texans and their attitudes, but the general point should already be clear. Population diversity means that Texans have many different attitudes about government and what its responsibilities should be. For that reason, the state is a more difficult place to govern than it was in times past, when the stereotypic Texan offered a fair example of what the majority of Texans desired from government.

New Governmental Realities: The Growth of Big Government

At the same time that there is less consensus among Texans today about the role of government, a considerable number of us still hold quite traditional attitudes on that matter—much like those of the stereotypic Texan discussed above. Traditional Texas values about government were rooted in individualism and favored a small government with limited responsibilities and low expenses. Many Texans still hold these attitudes today, but the days of small, limited government in Texas are long gone. Unfortunately, many Texans have not faced the reality of that fact, which hampers their efforts to understand government or control it through the democratic process.

Big government has come to Texas. The government budget and employment figures we cited previously offer some evidence for that. More evidence will be provided throughout this text as we describe the institutions and functions of our governments and how they affect our lives. But big government didn't appear overnight. It grew slowly during the twentieth century as Texans confronted one problem after another for which they desired government assistance. Public demands, in other words, were a principal cause of the growth of government. And the process "snowballed" as more and more responsibilities were added to government's agenda. The federal government has been a party to these developments, too, by forcing states to adopt a number of new programs and policies, especially since the 1960s.

Many Texans are uncomfortable with big government; some even fail to recognize its reality. Others would like to turn back the clock and reduce government to its former role and size. But we also act in contradictory ways that put new pressures on government to keep and even expand its responsibilities. Read virtually any daily newspaper and you will see evidence of that pressure. Here's one group of citizens demanding that our state or local governments do more to reduce crime. Here's another group demanding that government take more responsibility for environmental problems. Here's a state legislator or other elected official demanding that more effort be devoted to public education. Texans are constantly demanding that their governments take on more responsibilities, solve more problems, and inevitably spend more money in the process. Even those who claim they prefer a small, limited government have an agenda of problems they think the state should solve.

These contradictory attitudes and behaviors make governing the state far more difficult. Average citizens are, in effect, not always certain what role they want government to play, and for that reason they put contradictory pressures on government officials. The reality, however, is that we cannot turn back the clock. Big government is here to stay in Texas, as it is in every highly industrialized state and nation. A number of states have even bigger governments with more extensive responsibilities, but that fact is perhaps only of academic interest. Texans must learn to live with the inevitability of big government as it exists in our state.

New Policy Challenges

Unfortunately, there are also good reasons to believe that our state and local governments will grow even bigger—or that they will at least take on a number of new responsibilities in the near future. Our governments face a variety of problems today. Currently the state legislature has been grappling, in particular, with how to finance the public school system in an equitable manner, resolve the crisis in providing adequate prison space and alternative treatment for convicted felons, upgrade the state's mental health facilities to meet the requirements of a court order, revise the tax system to ensure adequate revenues, and formulate a budget to pay for these and other initiatives over the next biennium. And these problems are only the ones at the top of the legislature's list.

We are tempted to call these "catch-up" problems. They exist because of what the state has *not* done in prior years. It did not plan for adequate prison or mental health facilities, or it simply refused to do so because the cost appeared to be so high. It would not confront the inequities in school funding, prison facilities, or mental health services until forced to do so by the courts. It would not face a number of other problems either out of simple inertia or because of the anticipated cost of doing so. The state must now face many of these problems, and they will cost more to resolve because they were ignored in the past.

And while we grapple with those old problems, the state has to confront some new, perhaps even more important, ones. These new problems arise because natural-resource industries like oil and gas, which have traditionally been so important in Texas, are declining in their contribution to the economy. Our state and local governments are thus attempting to attract new firms and industries. They are especially interested in "high-tech" ones, which many people believe will be the most prominent in the future.

But all the other states and most foreign countries are trying to attract such firms. Thus our efforts to revitalize the state's economy face stiff competition. And there are other problems we must face because of these economic changes. How do we educate Texas schoolchildren and college students for the workplace of the twenty-first century? How do we retrain workers in declining industries for that new era? How do we diversify our economy so it will not be reliant on only one or two industries in the future as it was in the past? How do we get through what we hope will be the short-term difficulties of the transition from an industrial, oil-and gas-dependent economy to one based on some more advanced industries?

Thus our state has more than its share of "catch-up" problems, but it must also look to the future and grapple with even bigger, long-term policy challenges. How and how well the state deals with these problems will affect the quality of our lives and those of our children in a host of ways. The study of state and local government is not just an ivory-tower, intellectual exercise. It is relevant to the everyday life of all Texans. This book is written with that fact in mind. We survey the institutions and procedures of state government, as does every such text, but always with a view toward the effects of these matters on the average Texan, as will be pointed out throughout the text.

Summary

1. Texas is a physically large state with a diverse population. For these reasons alone it is also a particularly difficult state to govern.

2. The diversity of the state's population means that there are many different sets of attitudes about and expectations for government's responsibilities.

3. The size and diversity of the state's economy create more problems for government and a wide array of competing interests attempting to influence government policy.

4. Whereas Texas once had a small government with modest powers, its government today is large and has many, diverse responsibilities. While many Texans claim that they prefer limited government, they frequently demand that state and local governments take on new responsibilities.

5. Today, the state of Texas faces a number of challenging old and new policy problems. The old problems are ones we have grappled with for some time without success, while most of the new ones concern our economic future and the challenges we face to secure it.

References

JORDAN, TERRY G., JOHN L. BEAN, JR., AND WILLIAM M. HOLMES. 1984. *Texas: A Geography.* Boulder, Co.: Westview Press.

2

Race, Diversity, and Economic Change

There were 11,000 Hispanics in Texas in 1850. Today there are almost 4.5 million. Hispanics are, by far, the fastest-growing racial group in the state. From only 5 percent of the population in 1850 they have grown to account for 11 percent in 1920, 15 percent in 1960, 21 percent in 1980, and 26 percent in 1990. It is estimated that by the year 2000 they will constitute 36 percent of the population, and by 2025 they will account for 54 percent of the total population. In fact, in only a little more than two decades racial minorities will be the majority. Census projections indicate that by the year 2015 Hispanics will account for 40 percent of the population, blacks for 11 percent, and Asians and other minorities 6 percent. Anglos will clearly be in the minority, with only 44 percent.

These racial changes represent a fundamental transformation in the state. However, the emergence of Hispanics as a significant group could not have been anticipated from their share of the population in 1850. In fact, census figures for that year suggested that blacks rather than Hispanics would be the major minority group in the state. In that year, 59,000 of the total population of 213,000 Texans were black slaves. As noted, only 11,000 were Hispanic. But from a high of 28 percent of the population in 1850, the black share began a slow but steady erosion that continues today. In 1900, blacks accounted for 20 percent of the population, 16 percent in 1920, 14 percent in 1940, 12 percent in 1960, and only 12 percent today. While every third Texan will be a Hispanic in less than a decade, and every other Texan will be a Hispanic in less than thirty years, only one out of every ten Texans will be black.

In 1850; Texas had large numbers of blacks because of slavery. Before the Civil War, Anglo migrants from the Lower South states—Alabama, Georgia, Louisiana, and Mississippi—brought their slaves and plantation economy with them. They settled in East Texas and worked their cotton plantations with slave labor. It is no accident, therefore, that even today the great majority of blacks live in the eastern half of the state. It should also come as no surprise that blacks have never seen Texas as the promised land. After the Civil War, Texas didn't attract many black newcomers. The last substantial movement of blacks into the state was before the Civil War and that migration, of course, was an involuntary one. Actually, there were significant out-migrations of blacks in the decades of 1900–1910, 1940–1950, and 1950–1960. For example, Tom Bradley, the mayor of Los Angeles, was born in Calvert, Texas, at one time a thriving commercial and financial center for the great cotton plantations in the region. While Bradley was still a young boy, his parents moved to California in search of economic opportunity and a measure of political and social justice.

While blacks moved out, Anglos and Hispanics moved in. The Anglo migration into the state was particularly heavy during the economic boom of the 1960s, 1970s, and early 1980s. Although the depressed oil economy has slowed migration in recent years, the movement of newcomers into Texas continues at a significant rate. These newly arrived Anglos tend to be young, well-educated, and employed in white-collar and professional positions. Hispanic migrants from Mexico, on the other hand, are not well educated or well off. In fact, huge numbers enter the state illegally, and it is estimated that a million or more illegal aliens live in Texas.

While Anglos are not yet an endangered species, they will soon lose their position as the dominant majority in the state; in

---

some cities and regions they already have. In Houston, for example, blacks, Hispanics, and Asians constitute 63 percent of the population. Only one out of every three Houstonians is an Anglo. South Texas will be 80 percent Hispanic by the turn of the century. In addition, by the year 2000 Hispanics and blacks will account for half of the state's population aged thirty and younger. Given the enormous significance of racial minorities in Texas, and their increasing importance in the future, it is useful to explore their situation in some detail.

Ethnicity, Poverty, and Present-Day Politics

Blacks and Hispanics tend to be much poorer than Anglos. The percentage of all Texas children in poverty increased from 19 percent in 1979 to 25 percent in 1989, and much of this increase can be attributed to poverty in minority groups. The poverty rate of minority families is four times as high as that of Anglo families. One out of every four black and Hispanic families in Texas lives in poverty, while only one out of every twenty Anglo families earns an income below the poverty level.

Hispanics

The economic situation is actually deteriorating for many Hispanics. The poverty rate of Hispanics in Houston rose from 19 percent in 1980 to 30 percent in 1988. During this same period average Hispanic family income fell from $25,281 to only $19,000. Another startling statistic, indicative of the enormous problems in the minority community, is that 50 percent of all Hispanics entering public school will never graduate.

Increasingly, however, Hispanics recognize that political action can be used in an effort to improve their condition. Hispanic school districts played a major role in a recent state court decision that held that the system of financing public education in Texas was unconstitutional because it discriminated against poor districts. In 1988, Hispanics also filed a lawsuit alleging that the state discriminates against Hispanic students by providing fewer programs and giving less money to public colleges with large Hispanic enrollments. They also charged that the major universities in the state fail to enroll and graduate sufficient numbers of Hispanics. For examples, only 9 percent of the students at the University of Texas and only 5 percent at Texas A&M are Hispanic.

Hispanic leaders believe that better educational opportunities are fundamental to economic and political progress. They point out that while Hispanics account for 25 percent of high school graduates, they account for only 12 percent of the first-year students in senior colleges in the state. Anglos, on the other hand, account for 60 percent of high school graduates but 80 percent of the college first-year students. Obviously, Anglos are heavily overrepresented in terms of their share of college enrollments. Hispanics are heavily underrepresented.

The lawsuit also charges that the state spends considerably less money per student at predominantly Hispanic universities. Sixty percent of all Hispanics attending college are enrolled in institutions located in South Texas and El Paso. Expenditure per capita for higher education in the region is only $70, compared to a statewide average of $160. There are more than six hundred doctoral and professional degree programs offered by public universities in the state, yet only two are offered in the South Texas and El Paso areas. No public law schools or medical schools exist in the region.

If one believes that educational services and opportunities should be provided in large part on the basis of need, then it appears the South Texas region has been greatly deprived by the public authorities. The region has the lowest educational level in the state (9.7 years), the lowest per capita income, and the highest unemployment rate. However, it is one of the fastest-growing regions in the state, with three of the ten largest metropolitan areas (Corpus Christi, McAllen-Edinburg, and Brownsville-Harlingen).

Hispanics have also initiated challenges to local election systems. In Houston, where they comprise 28 percent of the population, they are underrepresented on the city council, commissioners court, and school board. Even though there are several hundred thousand Hispanics in the city, only one Hispanic sits on the fourteen member city council. Hispanics have also begun to demand more equitable representation in state government. Hispanics hold only 6 percent of the gubernatorial appointments to state boards and commissions, and less than one out of every ten state judges is Hispanic.

Blacks

Black Texans have made enormous progress since slavery was abolished in 1865. Once denied rights as human beings and considered property they now hold important positions in business, education, and government. Even as late as the 1950s and 1960s, black Texans were denied the right to vote; forced to attend segregated schools; discriminated against in employment, public accommodations, and housing; and frequently brutalized by the police. They were systematically excluded from the civic life of the state and community and relegated to menial jobs and tenant farming.

Much has changed. Legally, blacks now have access to full participation in the political life of the state. They can vote, organize interest groups to achieve their political goals, and run for political office. The doctrine of "separate but equal" educational systems for blacks and whites has long been unconstitutional and, in principle, black and white students attend the same schools. The Civil Rights Act of 1965 and other federal legislation, various executive orders of the president, and a variety of Supreme Court decisions during the past twenty-five years effectively struck down racially discriminatory state laws in the areas of housing, public and private accommodations, bank loans, employment, and public service provision. The "equal protection of the laws" section of the Fourteenth Amendment to the U.S. Constitution was also widely used by the Supreme Court in the 1960s to force the states to guarantee the civil liberties of black criminal defendants.

These laws and judicial decisions have effectively eliminated legal barriers to full black participation in the political, social, and economic life of the state. Blacks now vote in much greater numbers. Hundreds of blacks hold public office throughout the state as U.S. representatives; state representatives; federal, state, and municipal judges; prosecutors; mayors; city councilpersons; school board members; and county commissioners, clerks, and sheriffs. Thousands of blacks work as police officers, fire fighters, teachers, and professors. Hundreds more hold important executive positions as department heads, bureau chiefs, directors, chief deputies, and managers in city public works, building, planning, park and recreation, police, and fire departments. Black Texans no longer have to worry about being denied a table at a restaurant or a room at the Holiday Inn. Only thirty years ago, black children were forced to attend racially segregated schools; almost no blacks held either elected or appointed office; few served as police officers; and most, as a routine part of their daily lives, experienced legally sanctioned discrimination in employment, housing, and public accommodations. Therefore, the progress of the past three decades must be recognized as one of the great political and social accomplishments of our time.

On the other hand, the black community has such enormous problems that optimism about its future is unwarranted. What is happening to blacks in the country as a whole is also happening to blacks in Texas. Two separate black communities have developed. The figures are instructive. Nationally, in 1940, less than 190,000 blacks were employed in white-collar jobs, and a majority of these were as owners of small retail establishments in black neighborhoods, as clergymen, and as teachers in black schools. Fifty years later, almost two million blacks were employed as managers and professionals. During the period 1950–1990, the number of black citizens increased by 100 percent, but the number employed in white-collar occupations rose by over 900 percent. One segment of the black community has made remarkable progress in terms of income, education, social status, and education.

Unfortunately, that segment remains very small. Huge numbers of blacks live in a fundamentally different environment. In a nation with a population that is only 12 percent black, there are more black prison inmates than white or Hispanic ones. There are more black than white welfare recipients. A majority of black families is headed by women, and almost two out of every three black children are born to unmarried mothers. Forty percent of all black male high school dropouts in the 20–24 age group hold no job. The corresponding figures for whites and Hispanics are 12 percent and 10 percent, respectively. In an era when the importance of a college degree is increasing, black enrollments are declining.

The proportion of blacks in the 18–24 age group enrolled in college dropped from 23 percent to 21 percent during the period 1976–1988. The proportion of white college students increased from 27 percent to 31 percent. Another ominous sign is that by the late 1970s, black income levels were no longer catching up with white incomes. The wage differential between blacks and whites holds steady at 30 percent. These national patterns hold for Texas as well. In fact, it is almost certainly the case that on many of the indicators the situation for black Texans is even bleaker.

Race, Politics, and the Future

For all of its history as a republic and as a state, Texas has been white man's country—dominated by conservative white males of Anglo-Saxon descent. No group has yet been able to mount a serious and sustained challenge to their political and economic hegemony. Yet in only a few decades, Hispanics, blacks, and Asians will dominate, at least in terms of sheer numbers. And not long after that, Hispanics alone will enjoy a numerical majority. How will these traditional minorities, accustomed to a long history of subjugation, oppression, and racial exclusion, behave when they are finally in a position to express their political will? Will this "browning" of Texas rekindle racial hatred in the state's political and social life?

There is little in the state's past to suggest that political choices in the future will engender racial violence. For example, Texas escaped largely unscathed by the racial violence that swept Chicago, New York, Philadelphia, Los Angeles, and dozens of other major cities during the decade of the 1960s. Further, Anglos and Hispanics in Texas have long coexisted in peace if not in harmony in San Antonio, El Paso, and dozens of other cities throughout the state. At best, Texas has the opportunity to serve as an experiment in racial diversity and change. If the "browning" of the state's population, culture, and politics can be brought about peacefully, there is considerable cause for optimism regarding the racial changes that will inevitably transform the nation as a whole.

But just as race relations in the state have been relatively free of overt animosity and violence, there has never been any significant cultural interaction and exchange among the major ethnic groups. Texas was and remains a society strongly segregated on the basis of race and class. White, conservative Texans, accustomed to wealth, status, and power, will not easily relinquish the economic and political control enjoyed for generations. Yet the transformation of the social structure of the state will, at a minimum, challenge and perhaps overwhelm deeply entrenched assumptions and traditions about racial superiority. Old values based on an assumption of Anglo and Protestant dominance will only grudgingly give way to the encroachment of a Hispanic and Catholic culture. Inevitably, this confrontation will take place along a broad front. Already, we can dimly perceive the shape it may take.

Increasingly, the new majority will rely upon their newly found influence in the executive, legislative, and bureaucratic branches of government to press their grievances against the political system in areas such as public school finance, bilingual education, equal opportunity in employment, affirmative action, equitable representation on city councils and school boards, and police conduct. It is also likely that the new majority will invigorate competition between the major political parties. The emerging ethnic majority will demand greater public expenditures and responsibilities for education and social welfare services, which will in turn translate into higher taxes and an increased role for state and local governments. The tax system will be more progressive, government's regulatory and service provision roles will increase, and expenditures will grow. Texas will be more liberal than at any time in its history. The political system will be more open, accessible, and responsive to the diverse groups that will come to dominate the civic life of the state.

Unfortunately, other changes will be more ominous. It is likely that many white Texans will respond by accelerating past trends toward all-white, segregated suburban neighborhoods and private schools. Segregation will increase rather than decrease; racist attitudes may increase rather than wither away. The most bitter political struggles will incorporate racial overtones and appeals to racial bigotry. The conflicts will include political battles over welfare, crime, education, prisons, and taxes.

The next few decades will be momentous ones for Texans.

Race will play a major and even dominant role in the state's future and the issue has the potential to become a highly divisive one.

Economic Change

The past twenty-five years have borne witness to some of the most profound changes in the history of the state. The Texas of only a decade ago was dominated by oil, agriculture, and ranching. Cows, cotton, and crude fueled the economic engine. The population was concentrated in small towns and rural areas. Government was limited and service levels were either low or nonexistent. A tiny economic and political elite exerted tight control over the governmental apparatus and used public power to benefit the upper reaches of society. Racial discrimination and segregation were the norms in voting, housing, employment, accommodations, and education. The political, social, and economic system was closed and elitist. The state was economically backward, socially and culturally isolated, politically primitive, and racially repressed. At mid twentieth century, Texas looked as much to, and had as much in common with, the past century as it did with the present.

All of that would soon begin to change, slowly at first, and then with increasing speed. One major change has been economic. In 1940, over 30 percent of the state's labor force was employed in agriculture. Today, that figure is less than 3 percent and declining. The state's economy is now both diversified and industrialized. Huge numbers of Texans are employed in manufacturing jobs. Millions more work in wholesale and retail trades, government service, the professions, finance, insurance, real estate, and the transportation and communications sectors. Emerging sectors of the economy include various high-tech industries. The trend away from a dependence on oil and agriculture was given a powerful boost by the depression in the oil industry that crippled the state's economy during the 1980s.

Changes in Politics and Public Policy

Economic development and change also contributed to the dramatic growth of the state's great cities—Houston, Dallas, San

Antonio, and El Paso—and to fundamental changes in their politics and policies. An economy based on manufacturing and services requires urban locations. In turn, the tremendous growth of cities (80 percent of all Texans now live in urban areas) forced state and local governments to dramatically expand the number and level of public services and programs. Urban areas require extensive water and sewer systems, roads, bridges, freeways, schools, police and fire protection, sanitation, libraries, utilities, recreation, health and welfare services, regulation, and land-use planning. These services are enormously expensive. During the period 1960–1990, state and local governments in Texas were forced to dramatically increase their functional responsibilities. This great growth in the level, scope, and complexity of government resulted in more public employees and much higher expenditure levels. In turn, higher expenditures caused a significant increase in state and local taxes. And these are but a few examples of how "big government," as discussed in Chapter 1, has come to Texas.

The changes discussed above also exerted a major impact upon the political system in the state. As education and income levels improved, more people began to take an interest in what government was or was not doing. Increased interest in politics led a variety of groups to press their claims upon state and local governments. New groups—blacks, Hispanics, women, public employees, environmentalists—emerged to challenge the status quo. The closed, elitist system that had dominated Texas politics for generations began to open up. The establishment that had controlled the state since the nineteenth century began to crumble in the face of a variety of powerful forces—economic change, urbanization, migration, emerging minority groups, and a wealthier and better-educated population.

The one-party system that had dominated Texas since the Reconstruction period after the Civil War was unable to survive these profound changes. In the wake of the upheaval caused by various economic, social, and political transformations, the Republican Party emerged as a viable political organization. Democratic candidates no longer ran unopposed. The Democratic primary election outcome was no longer tantamount to victory. For the first time in a hundred years, the Republicans elected state senators, representatives, and even governors. They sent senators and representatives to Washington. The once-unbreakable grip of the Democrats on the political life of the state was shattered forever.

The courts also continue to play a key role in forcing the state's political authorities to come to grips with important problems. For example, a federal district court has required state officials to dramatically increase the amount of money spent on state prisons. Another court has forced the state to significantly increase spending on mental health and retardation services and programs. Further, a state district court recently found the state's system of funding public education to discriminate against poor school districts, and it ordered state officials to develop a more equitable system of public-school finance. The importance of the judiciary in Texas politics is further illustrated by the fact that for the past twenty years the federal courts have carefully scrutinized and frequently changed the local electoral system in Texas cities. In Houston and Dallas, the courts have held that the at-large method for electing members to the city council discriminates against racial minorities. They ruled that a mixed ward and at-large system is required.

Demographic Change and Public Policy

Even though the depressed price of oil during the period 1986–1989 threw the Texas economy into a tailspin, the state continued to grow during the 1980s. From 1980 to 1990, the population grew from 14,282,000 to about 17,000,000, an increase of about two and three-quarters of a million people. In fact, only one other state in the nation added more people than Texas. Texas is also the youngest of the ten largest states. It has the largest percentage of residents under twenty-five years of age (40.6 percent) and the smallest percentage of those forty-five years and older (26.5 percent).

Texas, therefore, is one of the largest, youngest, and fastest-growing states in the nation. It not only has one of the country's largest state economies, it has one of the *world's* largest economies. However, the state ranks an abysmal forty-seventh among the fifty states in adult literacy. Twenty percent of all adults in Texas are illiterate. Further, many Texans are poor and unable to provide even basic food, clothing, shelter, and health care for their families. Despite its large poor and illiterate population, the state of Texas provides remarkably modest public services to assist such people, as we will explain in detail in Chapter 15. Texas is one of the least generous states in the provision of welfare benefits, public health services, and social services generally. Even public education is relatively poorly funded. However, the powerful forces changing Texas society suggest that government will continue to grow and that we will see frequent and bitter political battles in the future between those who favor a traditional role for government and those who favor an activist one.

Summary

1. Hispanics are the fastest-growing racial group in the state. They accounted for 26 percent of the population in 1990, and it is estimated that they will constitute 36 percent of the state's population by the year 2000.

2. The poverty rate of black and Hispanic families is four times as high as that of Anglo families. While only one out of every twenty Anglo families earns an income below the poverty level, one out of every four minority families in Texas lives in poverty.

3. National laws and judicial decisions have effectively eliminated legal barriers to full participation on the part of black citizens in the political life of the state.

4. As black and Hispanic groups grow in strength and numbers, they will demand greater public expenditures for education and social welfare services. These higher service levels and expenditures will translate into higher taxes and an increased role for state and local governments.

5. The powerful forces of economic change, urbanization, migration, and a wealthier and better-educated population have caused a variety of new groups—racial minorities, women, and public employees—to challenge the status quo.

The result has been an opening up of the closed, elitist system that has dominated Texas politics for generations.

6. Although Texas is one of the largest, youngest, and fastest-growing states in the nation, it is one of the least generous in the provision of welfare benefits, public health services, and social services generally.

3

The Constitutions of Texas

A constitution lays out the powers that a government may exercise and the principal organizational structures through which it may employ those powers. Thus if we know the essential details of a constitution, we will know as well what kind of government can exist under it.

The U.S. Constitution

The highest law of the land in Texas is the Constitution of the United States, ratified in 1789. That document is the fundamental law of the entire United States of America. It provides for a division of powers between the federal government and the governments of the states, describes the basic structure of the federal government, and places limits on the powers of both state and federal governments. The first and the last of these three functions of the Constitution are especially important to Texas and to Texans.

The Constitution indicates the principal role of both the state and federal governments, reserving some powers for each level. For example, the federal government has the exclusive power, among other things, to conduct foreign relations, declare war, and regulate foreign and interstate commerce. The Constitution also offers relatively broad definitions of the full set of powers granted the federal government. That fact has allowed presidents, the Congress, and the Supreme Court to expand remarkably the responsibilities of the federal government over the history of our nation. Many powers the federal government did not exercise early in the history of the nation have been found to be constitutional in later times because they could be justified under these broad definitions. Thus the U.S. Constitution has proved to be a flexible statement of federal government powers, allowing those powers to grow with changing conceptions of the role of government.

State government powers are not described in detail in the Constitution, but instead are indicated by the "residual powers" clause in the Tenth Amendment, which states: "The powers not delegated to the United States [government] by the Constitution, nor prohibited by it to the states, are reserved to the states respectively, or to the people." In practice, the states had preponderant control over most aspects of domestic government policy at the time the Constitution was adopted.

The Constitution's flexibility has been demonstrated most notably in the twentieth century. This century has witnessed a remarkable increase in public expectations for governmental responsibility. The flexibility of the Constitution has allowed the federal government to respond aggressively to those new expectations. In the process, the federal government has also assumed power in many areas traditionally reserved to the states. Thus the original division of powers between the states and the federal government has been radically changed over the course of American history.

While the growth of the federal government has reduced state powers in many areas, it has also expanded those powers in others. Federal government initiatives have often created policy partnerships with the states, making both levels of government more powerful than they were before. In addition, the twentieth century has witnessed a general expansion in the powers of all levels of governments. Thus, while the balance of power between the federal and the state governments has evolved, both levels have become far more powerful.

At the same time, the growth of federal government power

has slowed if not come to an end since 1980. Both presidents Ronald Reagan and George Bush sought to return more power to the states. Efforts to eliminate the federal budget deficit have also forced the scaling back of federal activities in recent years, leaving more responsibilities for state and local governments. Thus the balance of powers between these two levels of government is swinging back toward a greater state role.

Finally, we should observe that the U.S. Constitution imposes a number of restrictions on the powers of state and local governments. The principal restrictions are those of the Bill of Rights, which enumerate a number of specific guarantees of individual rights (freedom of speech, the press, of religion, and so on). In addition, various subsequent amendments to the Constitution have added other individual rights guarantees. Because of these provisions, the Constitution has become an important and frequently employed vehicle by which various Texans have sought legal recourse against their state or local government.

The Texas Constitution

The second-highest source of law in Texas is the state's own constitution, which was adopted in 1876. In certain respects our state constitution is quite similar to the federal one. It provides for a government whose power is based on public assent. It lays out a number of individual rights guarantees. And it requires a structure for the state government that is quite similar to that of the national government. There are separate executive, legislative, and judicial branches; a two-house legislature; and what appears to be one chief executive—the governor—in the executive branch.

Yet in several respects our state constitution is radically different from the national one. In part that is the case because all state constitutions serve a distinctive purpose. The national Constitution is the source of all governmental power in the United States and, as noted above, it makes a broad and unspecific grant of power to the states. State constitutions, then, must indicate how that broad grant of power is to be limited. They do not confer powers on the state's governments; instead they lay out the desired restrictions on those powers that are granted by the national Constitution. Without those restrictions the state's

---

elected officials would have the opportunity to shape government policy as they desired. For this reason the writers of most state constitutions have produced detailed, specific documents with careful attention to limits on governmental power.

And the authors of the Texas constitution were particularly desirous of restricting the powers of state government. They were reacting to their unhappy experiences under a strong state government ruled by "Yankees and carpetbaggers" during Reconstruction after the Civil War. Thus they sharply reduced the powers of the governor and state legislature and reduced the state's powers to raise tax revenues and spend money on public programs. The constitution is, in effect, a laundry list of limitations on governmental power, and the authors of the document were so zealous in their efforts that the list is an incredibly long one. Yet while the authors of our constitution were good at detail, they were hopeless with organization. As a result, our constitution is not only long and highly specific, it is also a convoluted, ill-organized, forbiddingly written document. As bedside reading, it would be a Texas-sized sleeping pill.

The Effects of the State Constitution

The authors of our state constitution created a government well suited for their own times and for public preferences at the time. Unfortunately, they were so successful in that effort that we still largely have that same governmental system today, when public demands on government have changed dramatically. Even in Texas, with an essentially conservative citizenry, our state and local governments must grapple with a range of complicated and controversial policies far beyond the imagination of the men who wrote our constitution. As a result, we have a nineteenth-century government that must contend with late twentieth-century problems.

The Texas constitution narrowly restricts the taxing and spending powers of both state and local governments. The governor is so restricted in his or her powers as to be more a figurehead than a true chief executive. The legislature is equally limited by constitutional restrictions that make it a part-time, amateur body allowed to meet only for brief sessions every two years. Finally, both the executive and judicial branches are ill organized, with complicated, duplicative structures. Thus they are inefficient on the one hand and difficult for the average citizen to understand on the other.

The Evolution of the Texas Constitution

In certain respects we do not live today under the same constitution that was promulgated in 1876. It has been changed many times through the amendment process. But not all that change has been for the good, and the document is not remarkably improved as a result.

A lengthy, detailed, highly restrictive constitution inevitably requires frequent revision as the demands on government change. And Texans have faced up to that fact. We have changed our state constitution with over three hundred amendments since it was adopted, roughly tripling the length of the document from the time it was adopted. (Over five hundred amendments have been proposed for adoption by the voters over its life.) In recent state elections voters have often faced eight to twelve proposed amendments on the ballot.

The constitution itself provides for this amendment process. A proposed amendment must be adopted, first, by two-thirds of the full membership of each house of the Texas Legislature. Then it must be approved by a majority of those people voting in a forthcoming general or special election.

But all these amendments, once again, do not necessarily mean the document has been dramatically improved. Many amendments arise when a narrow, specific restriction of the constitution prevents the state from implementing a desired new policy. But the typical way of handling this situation has been to draft a proposed amendment that itself only allows a narrow, specific grant of power for that particular new policy. The general sense of restrictiveness is retained. Equally frequently, special-interest groups have used the amendment process to get special concessions into the constitution. Many special interests recognize that a provision in constitutional law is "safer," or more difficult to erase, than one merely in a law passed by the legislature. Thus the state constitution is today littered with such provisions adopted through the amendment process.

For these reasons the constitution is not remarkably im-

Examples of Special-Interest Constitutional Provisions

Article VIII of the Texas Constitution on "Taxation and Revenue" offers a number of good examples of special-interest provisions. Article VIII begins with the statement that "all real property and tangible personal property in this State, whether owned by natural persons or corporations, other than municipal [that is, municipal corporations or cities], shall be taxed in proportion to its value."

At subsequent points in Article VIII, however, the following particularly notable categories of property are awarded exemptions, reductions, or "tax breaks"—all of which were added by constitutional amendments.

Personal residences, through a "homestead exemption," or a reduction in the total value of a personal residence which will be subject to local property taxes

Agricultural land used exclusively for agricultural purposes

Farm products, livestock, and poultry in the hands of the producer, and family supplies for home and farm use

Farming implements ("implements of husbandry") that are used in the production of farm or ranch products

Solar- or wind-powered energy devices

Mobile marine drilling equipment designed for offshore drilling of oil and gas wells that is being stored while not in use in a county bordering on the Gulf of Mexico

Property owned by a disabled veteran or the surviving spouse and surviving minor child of a disabled veteran

Some and perhaps all of these tax breaks may constitute good tax policy, or they may be wise ways to achieve various other goals through tax policy. Whether they should be included in the constitution instead of statutory law is another matter. But what is undeniably clear is that these special interests, and others that have been secured in the constitution, are especially well protected from future legal changes.

proved despite a hundred years of scrutiny and more than three hundred amendments. A bit of fine-tuning has been enacted, and the minimal concessions to new state powers and responsibilities have been made, yet the essential philosophy and the most important restrictions of the original version are intact.

The constitution also provides for the possibility of wholesale revision. If the citizens of Texas so desired, we could replace the entire document by creating a constitutional convention charged with drafting a new one for voter approval. Yet the three most vigorous efforts to do so, in 1917, in 1919, and from 1972 to 1975 all failed. Only in the last of these instances was a proposed new constitution actually brought before the electorate, and it was soundly defeated. The failure of the last effort was particularly unfortunate. The proposed new constitution was widely endorsed by legal scholars, civic groups, and a number of prominent Texans of both political parties. But the opposition of a host of special-interest groups and of then-Governor Dolph Briscoe, coupled with a poor public-education effort by the supporters of the new document, led to its defeat.

There is another lesson of the constitutional revision effort from 1972 to 1975. Debates about constitutional law are not exciting or even very interesting for the average voter. The constitution has harmful effects on state government, but they are complicated and a bit esoteric. Further, the conservatism of average Texans make them mistrustful of any change that might possibly enlarge government power. Thus we must conclude that it will be difficult to marshall notable public support for correcting the flaws of our present constitutional system. The one we have, warts and all, will be with us for some time to come.

Summary

1. The U.S. Constitution defines the roles and powers of the states and the federal government. It is the highest law of the nation to which all other federal, state, and local laws must conform.

2. When it was first adopted, the Constitution left the principal responsibility for domestic policy problems to the states. Over American history, however, evolving interpretations

of the Constitution have allowed the federal government to become the dominant partner in the federal system. Yet the states have also grown remarkably more powerful during this period.

3. The Texas Constitution is superficially similar to the U.S. Constitution, but it is a rigid instead of a flexible document. For that reason it sharply restricts the state's ability to respond to changing political problems and public demands.

4. The Texas Constitution has been amended more than three hundred times, but its basic restrictive character remains unchanged and its deficiencies have been little improved.

5. The Texas constitution also contains a large number of provisions that protect special interests and, in effect, restrict further the power of state and local governments, especially when making policies that affect those special interests.

4

Political Parties in Texas

Political parties are traditionally considered critical to the functioning of modern democratic governments. Parties recruit candidates for office and help those individuals organize and run their campaigns. Parties assist the government in administering the election process, and they attempt to mobilize voters to support the candidates running under their label. Once elected to office, the members of a given party try to work together to pursue their common policy goals.

Thus parties help carry out some of the mechanical tasks associated with the democratic process. And they provide a means by which like-minded Texans can join together to influence government policy. They help individual Texans control and direct the actions of our state and local governments.

Parties as Organizations

The preceding recitation of what parties do emphasizes their organizational activities, and that is one useful way to think about these groups. We typically think of parties, as well, as strictly private organizations, but that is no longer entirely accurate. Government has recognized the essential roles that parties play in the democratic process and to ensure that those roles are fairly executed, state laws regulate parties quite closely. These laws proscribe the organizational structure of parties, indicate how they may nominate candidates for election to public office, regulate primary and general election processes, and even dictate many of the campaign finance procedures that candidates and parties must follow. Thus political parties can be thought of as "quasi-public" organizations. Alternatively, one can think of them as highly regulated organizations, much like many business organizations that are also highly regulated by government today.

The most detailed state regulations and requirements are effectively imposed on just the Democratic and Republican parties, because the requirements are for those parties whose candidates for governor received at least 20 percent of the votes in the last general election. (Smaller parties are not required to have as extensive an organizational structure, and they can nominate candidates for office at conventions instead of by primary elections.) State law requires, first, that these two dominant parties have a permanent set of officers. At the top is the state executive committee, the highest party leaders and strategists. Below that, there are district executive committees (in counties that have more than one state senate district) and county executive committees (in all other counties). Further, there are elected county and precinct chairpersons.

State law also requires the Democrats and Republicans to choose their nominees for public office in primary elections, in the spring of the year of the general elections. The various party officials and committees are responsible for arranging primary election and convention procedures at their particular levels of the organization. They are also involved in recruiting candidates to run for election and in soliciting campaign funds for those candidates. Thus these officers and committees can work year round, at least as necessary, to keep the party functioning.

During election years, a second phase of party organization comes into action—the party's conventions, where the membership at large can participate. On the evening of the primary election, active party members attend precinct conventions, principally to elect delegates to the county-level convention. The major task before the county meeting is to elect delegates to the state convention. At both the precinct and county meetings various factions of the party attempt to control the meeting, elect their members to the next higher convention, and get the meeting to endorse their public policy goals.

The state convention's principal goal is to adopt a platform of principles and policy positions. Thus the debate about proposals for new government policies continues here and is settled when the convention delegates endorse a platform. In a sense, too, this convention is a pep rally for the parties' candidates for office who were selected earlier in the year in the primary election.

Many people believe that there are few differences between the two major parties, but the platforms that their members author at these conventions offer testimony to the contrary. The 1990 platforms of the state's Democratic and Republican parties indicate good examples of substantial differences in policy preferences. The accompanying table lists some of the most obvious examples, for policy questions where the two parties both clearly stated a position. Other differences are indicated on policy issues where only one party expressed its position. The Democrats call for greater government responsibility and action on a number of civil rights and social welfare issues in particular. Clearly, these positions and those listed in the table indicate a decidedly liberal orientation.

The Republicans went on record as favoring capital punishment, prayer in public schools by constitutional amendment, and the teaching of a "balanced view of the origin of life" in public schools, instead of just the theory of scientific evolution. In addition, the Republicans opposed gun control by the government and asked for government efforts to restrict homosexual conduct and behavior, because they saw homosexuality as a threat to the family as well as a contributor to the spread of AIDS. Clearly, the Republicans adopted a very conservative platform, and the two parties are remarkably different in their policy preferences expressed at the conventions.

Notable Policy Differences in the 1990 Platforms of the State Democratic and Republican Parties

Democrats	*Republicans*

Abortion

"Pro-choice." Wish to let the individual woman decide. Want family planning services for all citizens.	"Right to life." Want constitutional protection for the unborn. Opposed to the use of government funds for abortions.

Bilingual Education Programs

Favor	Oppose

Family Planning and Contraception Information for Minors

Favor	Oppose

Universal Health Care Program

Favor, by federal government action	Oppose

Welfare Programs

Want catastrophic health insurance, extension of Medicaid program for the poor, and more aid for the elderly, chronically ill, and disabled.	Support private initiatives instead of government programs. Want to stop "handouts" to the able-bodied on welfare. Want aid restricted to the aged, handicapped, and truly needy.

The Party Membership

Who are the members of the parties and how does one become one? These are unusual organizations because there are very few "card-carrying" members and only very modest restrictions that govern membership. And there are even two kinds of party "members." If one wishes to be an active member of a party and participate in its organizational activities, the principal way is to begin by attending a precinct convention on the evening of the primary election. To participate in the activities of that convention, one must reside in the precinct and have voted in that party's primary. By regular participation in such meetings one might become an officer or a delegate to higher-level conventions. And simply attending any precinct convention allows one to participate in debates about the public policy preferences of the party at that level.

Thus the readers of this book who wish to influence a party's politics and issue positions might exert such influence by getting involved in the precinct organization we've described. By regular involvement in the precinct organization one might be chosen as a state convention delegate as well.

Those who attend these conventions and get involved in the party organization are labeled party activists by political scientists. Party activists are likely to be involved in a number of related party functions at the same time. Most typically, they will assist one or more candidates for office in their election campaigns. Some of them have aspirations for becoming party officers or candidates for elected office themselves.

Yet there is another level of party membership that requires little active effort. We might call the members of this second level the party followers, or the party identifiers, as they are known in the political science literature. This second level includes the vast majority of Texans. In fact, the only requirement to be a party follower is that one personally identify with a party, one of its candidates for office, or the policy goals of the party or candidate. And the majority of Texans does identify in this fashion with one of the two major parties. In recent years approximately 30 percent of the voting-age Texans claim allegiance to the Republican party, about 30 percent also claim allegiance to the Democrats, and 30 percent profess to being independents.

(The remainder express neither a party preference nor a clear sense of self-identification as an independent.)

Do the Parties Differ in Their Membership?

Many people believe that the major parties are not very different from one another in their membership, especially in Texas, where both parties have traditionally been quite conservative. But one can see notable differences between the two among both their party identifiers and party activities.

Party Identifiers

Recent public opinion polls provide evidence on how party identifiers in Texas differ. Table 4.1 from a 1991 poll lists selected, prominent characteristics that illustrate some of those differences. The majority of both parties, and of the independents for that matter, is made up of Anglos between thirty and forty-four years old whose annual income is between $20,000 and $40,000. Yet the Democratic Party attracts far more older, ethnic minority, poorer, and liberal Texans. The Republican Party has remarkably many conservative, wealthy, and younger identifiers. At the same time, it has remarkably few black or Hispanic ones. As a group, the independents fall between the two major parties on most of these characteristics, but they are more similar to the Democrats than the Republicans in terms of ethnicity, income, and ideology.

Party Activists

Party activists share many things in common with party followers, but they are also quite distinctive in several ways. A particularly good description of Texas party activists comes from a study of such people in the Democratic and Republican parties in Houston. The authors of that study say of these activists,

> As one might expect with people who volunteer much time and effort for little or no financial reward, the parties in Houston both attract men and women with the

TABLE 4.1 Selected Characteristics of Party Identifiers

	Democrats	*Independents*	*Republicans*
Percentage of each party's members whose ages are between:			
18–29	18	20	23
30–44	34	37	41
45–61	22	24	23
62–95	26	19	14
Percentage of each party's members whose ethnicity is:			
Anglo	57	77	89
Black	19	6	1
Hispanic	21	14	7
Other	2	4	3
Percentage of each party's members whose annual income is between:			
$0–20,000	21	19	13
$20,001–40,000	55	49	38
$40,001–60,000	9	17	23
$60,001 +	9	8	19
Not Ascertained	5	7	7
Percentage of each party's members who claim they are:			
Liberals	22	17	8
Moderates	42	43	34
Conservatives	27	34	54
Not Ascertained	8	6	4

Source: The Texas Poll was conducted by Harte-Hanks Communications, Inc. and the Public Policy Research Laboratory of Texas A&M University.

time and financial resources to afford politics, the information to understand it, and the skills to be useful.

[But] Republican precinct leaders, compared with Democrats, are older, drawn more from professional and technical fields, have higher incomes, are more likely to be married and almost universally are white.

The Democrats are more typical of the general population. Blacks are represented in approximate proportion to their numbers in the population. There is also a noticeable minority of Democratic workers with low levels of formal education, income, and job status, as well as more retired persons. (Murray and Tedin, 1986:46)

Thus party activists are generally more educated and better off financially than the average Texan, but Democratic activists are less so than Republicans and are more like the general population in these respects and in ethnicity. If we recall that it is these party activists who write the platforms at the conventions, and if we recall the character of those platforms as discussed earlier, it is also fair to conclude that activists are likely to be more extremist in their ideological views than are other Texans. Democratic activists, that is, are especially likely to be liberal and Republican ones are especially likely to be conservative.

Is Texas a Two-Party State?

For most of the twentieth century, Texas was a solidly one-party state, with the Democrats in near-total control of state and local government. Beginning in the early 1950s, however, the Republican Party began to make steady if slow progress in its effort to compete with the Democrats. In some respects that progress has led to a two-party state, but in other respects it has not.

If one considers the levels of party support in the general public as indicated by the numbers of party identifiers, the two parties are essentially equal in size. There are no comparative numbers of party activists, so we cannot compare the two at that level. But we can compare how successful the two parties have

Chapter 4

been in actually attracting voter support and controlling elected government offices.

Since 1978, Democratic and Republican candidates have competed on virtually equal footing for the governorship, actually swapping control of the office at each election. Democrats still win most, if not all, of the other state-level elective offices, like those for the lieutenant governor, attorney general, comptroller, and so on. But Republicans seem to become more competitive in each succeeding election for these offices. In similar fashion, while the Republican Party has made steady progress in other major elections in the state, they still hold a minority of most offices. After the 1990 election, for example, the Democrats held ninety-four of the one hundred fifty seats in the Texas House of Representatives, and twenty-one of the thirty-one seats in the Texas Senate. Likewise, Republicans held one of the state's U.S. Senate seats and eight of the state's twenty-seven seats in the U.S. House of Representatives.

Thus one's conclusion about whether or not Texas is a two-party state depends on which level or kind of public support, or which measure of success in elections, one chooses to consider. What is clear, however, is that the Republican Party is far more successful today than in times past, and that it runs credible, competitive candidates for a large number of federal, state, and local offices. The Republican threat is sufficiently large that Democratic candidates have to take it seriously in most races.

Summary

1. Political parties are quasi-public organizations that play important roles in helping the state government implement the election process.

2. Parties help organize like-minded Texans, too, to control state government and its policy efforts. Parties also provide opportunities for individual Texans to get directly involved in this effort.

3. The two major parties attract notably different groups of followers and activists with equally different political pref-

erences. The Democrats are generally liberal, while the Republicans are generally conservative.

4. Texas has made remarkable progress toward two-party politics in the last generation, but the exact extent of that progress is still debatable.

References

MURRAY, RICHARD W. AND KENT L. TEDIN. 1986. "The Emergence of Two-Party Competition in the Sunbelt: The Case of Houston," pp. 39–63 in William Crotty (ed.). *Political Parties in Local Areas.* Knoxville: University of Tennessee Press.

5

State and Local Interest Groups

In a democratic society interest groups are supposed to help citizens influence the government much as political parties do. Interest groups do not run candidates for office, but they attempt to influence the policy preferences of candidates for office and of those individuals who are elected. In nondemocratic societies the right to form such groups and press policy demands on government is sharply limited. Americans, and Texans, are fortunate to have this right.

Yet interest groups are controversial participants in the governing process. Most scholars who study Texas government and a good number of average citizens, too, have a very critical view of how these organizations work and whose interests they represent. That critical view is well expressed by Frances T. Farenthold (1991), a former state legislator and unsuccessful candidate for governor in 1972 and 1974. She says:

> When I speak here of lobbyists . . . I refer to "the lobby within the lobby." This elite group—and I use the term advisedly—is composed of representatives of powerful business associations, former legislators selected for

their acumen, and the bright and able lawyers of presti-
gious law firms.

Members of this group are methodical, experienced, and untiring. They are permanent participants in the Texas legislative process, from the selection of candidates to their election, re-election, and defeat. By and large, they are not flamboyant. We do not read about them in the paper often. They have resources to draft legislation, select sponsors, and guide bills through passage and signing by the governor. They can stop legislation in its tracks, in a dozen different ways, or so compromise a bill by amendments that it retains only its original title.

Thus interest groups are acknowledged in this critical view to be very powerful, but only in the service of select, big-business groups.

Interest Groups Prominent in State Politics

As recently as a generation ago a very small number of un-usually powerful business groups did indeed dominate Texas politics. The oil and gas industry, agriculture, and banking, in particular, were among those especially powerful groups and organizations. Those traditionally dominant groups are still very powerful but they do not control state policymaking as they once did. They are themselves relatively weaker and many other groups and interests now compete with them to influence government policy. In part this is the case because a very large number of interest groups is active in Texas politics today. In fact, over the last twenty or so years there has been dramatic growth in the number of interest groups participating in American politics generally.

Yet some groups are still remarkably more powerful than their competitors. A recent study of interest groups in Texas politics, for example, concluded that five groups were far more powerful than any others. These "elite" groups included the Texas Trial Lawyers Association, the Texas Medical Society, the Texas Realtors Association, the Texas State Teachers Association, and the "big oil" lobby, which is principally represented by the Midcontinent Oil and Gas Association (Hamm and Wiggins, forthcoming).

This study also identified a "second team" of especially powerful interests that ranked just below the top five. This second group included the Texas Motor Truck Association, the Texas AFL-CIO, the Independent Oil and Gas Producers Association, the Texas Chemical Council, the Texas Association of Business, and the Texas Savings and Loan Association.

Doubtless, any rating of the most powerful interest groups will itself be controversial. The leaders and members of all the groups listed above would probably discount their power, but they would surely do so because truly powerful interest groups can suffer a negative public image. Further, a large number of small, less-known groups may be as influential as the "elite" on some occasions or with respect to seemingly modest aspects of government policy that greatly affect their particular group. But a host of scholarly and journalistic studies have argued that some groups are indeed far more powerful than others in Texas. And those studies have frequently named the groups listed here as enjoying unusual power.

Interest Groups Prominent in Local Politics

The interest groups involved with city or county politics will be largely "home grown" or strictly local groups. Thus they will differ from city to city and county to county. But a few notable interests will commonly be active in local politics. Local business interests, such as those in banking, construction, and real estate, in particular, will be highly involved in local politics. All these businesses are especially dependent on the health of the local economy, the "business image" of the city, and thus the ways local governments can contribute to those economic goals.

Other organized groups that are frequently active in local politics include associations of taxpayers that typically lobby against tax increases; neighborhood associations that work for policies to preserve the character and quality of neighborhood life; and public employee associations, such as those for police officers, firemen, and other city or county workers. The latter occupational associations typically lobby government and candidates for local office with regard to pay and other employment benefits.

A Group for Every Interest?

At this point some of our readers might wish to ask, "Who represents me?" They might also assume that the particular groups we have mentioned so far in this chapter only represent other people's interests. And they might wonder whether any groups lobby government on matters they care about. Yet we suspect that virtually every reader of this book has preferences for government policy that are supported by one or more active interest groups. Consider a few examples of how that might be the case.

The typical reader of this book is a college student seeking an education to advance his or her future career. A large number of those anticipated careers are also ones that state and local governments regulate in one or more respects. If one wishes to become, for example, an architect, insurance agent, lawyer, physician, police officer, public accountant, real estate agent or broker, or teacher, one's future profession is somehow regulated by the state. And there is a professional association for each one of these occupations that lobbies state and sometimes local government in the interests of that profession. And there are a good many more such regulated occupations and professions, as we will explain in Chapter 13, all with their own lobby organizations. When someone enters one of these professions in the future, he or she will be represented by the appropriate interest group. Even some of the work of those groups today is surely beneficial as well to future members of the profession. Thus many college students could identify the organization that lobbies for their intended profession and learn about the public policy interests of that organization.

Many other college students do not anticipate a career in one of the preceding professions, but they will work in industries like banking, insurance, oil and gas production or refining, transportation, or health care. All of these industries and a good many others are also regulated by state and local government.

And all these industries have one or more formal organizations that lobby these governments to influence the character of the regulations within which they must operate.

No doubt many college students are also interested in one or more issues of social or environmental policy for which state and local governments have responsibility. In the table "Social and Environmental Policy Issues and Interest Groups," we list a number of issues and the principal groups that lobby Texas governments on those matters. Most of these groups have Austin headquarters, and some of them have chapters in major cities or on college campuses. We encourage readers interested in these issues to learn more about the work of the relevant groups. And we know, as well, that this is only a sampling of the many policy issues, and hence interest groups, that might be of concern to our readers.

Finally, some readers might say that their concern is simply with good government. They want an interest group that lobbies for the average citizen on a variety of issues and works for honest, efficient, democratic government. They might even fear that all the other interest groups we have been discussing can at times shape state or local government policy in ways contrary to the general public interest. Such readers might want an organization whose goal is to fight against that possibility.

Common Cause of Texas, an organization headquartered in Austin, claims these very goals. Common Cause lobbies state and local government for honest, democratic government with restrictions on special-interest power. In recent years, as examples, Common Cause has lobbied for tighter restrictions on special-interest lobbying of government, more restrictive campaign finance laws, limits on special-interest influence, and tougher ethics for public officials.

How Interest Groups Influence Government

We have referred several times to how interest groups lobby government with regard to their interests, but these groups actually may carry on a host of activities to influence government policy. Perhaps, the most important political activities of interest

Social and Environmental Policy Issues and Interest Groups

A Selection of Prominent Policy Issues and Major Interest Groups
Active on Each Issue

Abortion policy	Planned Parenthood ("pro-choice," offices in many cities)
	Right to Life Advocates ("pro-life," Houston)
	Texas Abortion Rights Action League ("pro-choice," headquartered in Austin)
	Texas Right to Life ("pro-life," various cities)
Black Texans' rights	National Association for the Advancement of Colored People (various cities)
Consumer's rights	Texas Consumer Association (Austin)
	Consumers Union (Southwest Regional office in Austin)
Drunk driving	Mothers Against Drunk Driving (national office in Dallas; chapters in various cities)
Environmental policy	Audubon Society (various cities)
	Clean Water Action (Austin)
	Gulf Coast Conservation Association (Houston)
	Sierra Club (state office in Austin; Southern Plains regional office in Dallas; some chapters in other cities)
Gay rights	Lesbian–Gay Rights Lobby of Texas (Austin)

Hispanics' rights	League of United Latin American Citizens (San Antonio)
Individual rights	American Civil Liberties Union (various cities)
Mental illness and the rights of the mentally ill	Texas Alliance for the Mentally Ill (Austin)
Retarded persons' rights	Association for Retarded Citizens (various cities)
Women's rights	Texas Woman's Political Caucus (Austin)

groups would include their efforts to:

Recruit people sympathetic to the group's interests to run for public office.

Contribute money and volunteer time to the election campaigns of individuals sympathetic to the group. (Many interest groups also maintain political action committees or PACs, which are discussed in Chapter 6, as the mechanisms for funneling their campaign contributions to candidates.)

Lobby elected officials in a host of ways, using everything from polite encouragement to angry and vigorous threats of unfortunate electoral consequences, to gain their support.

Supply public officials with public policy research that supports the views and interests of the group.

Lobby the general public with newspaper advertisements or even use public demonstrations to evoke general public support for their cause.

Clever, aggressive, and well-financed interest groups, in particular, will use the bulk of these techniques to press their claims on government. Yet even small organizations with a core of dedicated individuals willing to work hard can use a number of them, too.

Summary

1. At one time, Texas politics was dominated by a select few, very powerful private-interest groups, including those representing the oil and gas industry, agriculture, and banking.

2. Today, more interest groups are active and share power, but some remain far more influential than others. Oil and gas interests, lawyers, physicians, teachers, and realtors are claimed by some to be among the most powerful today.

3. We often fear that interest groups might divert government from following the general public will, and indeed there is that risk. Yet we should recognize that our own preferences are often represented by such groups.

4. Interest groups use a variety of techniques to press their claims on government. A large organization or a well-funded one can be particularly aggressive in using these techniques. But even small groups can lobby successfully if they have the willpower and commitment of their members.

References

FARENTHOLD, FRANCES T. 1991. "Did Sharpstown Even Matter?" *The Houston Post,* January 13, 1991, C1.

HAMM, KEITH E. AND CHARLES W. WIGGINS. Forthcoming. "Texas: The Transformation from Personal to Informational Lobbying," in Ronald J. Hrebenar and Clive S. Thomas (eds.). *Interest Politics in the Southern States.* Tuscaloosa, Ala.: University of Alabama Press.

6

Elections

Elections are the most important part of the democratic process. It is here, of course, that we choose the people who will make our government policies. Elections also permit a crude but important form of communication between citizens and elected officials. We hope to indicate at least some of our preferences for government policy through our selection of candidates. Simultaneously, candidates, political parties, and interest groups hope to attract us to their causes. Thus elections are contests among a number of individuals and groups to shape government policy. How well elections work as instruments of democracy—whether the public "wins" the contest—depends on the rules by which elections operate, who participates, and how they do so.

The Rules for the Election Process

State laws govern almost every aspect of the election "game," so to play it you need to know the rules. State laws determine, first, the basic character of elections and who can participate in them. The following essential aspects of elections are regulated by state law.

The Nomination of Candidates

The nominees for public office put forward by political parties must be chosen by the procedures described in Chapter 4.

These procedures typically control the selection of the vast majority of nominees for statewide offices like the governorship, the state legislature, county offices, the U.S. Congress, and the presidency. Recalling the discussion in Chapter 4, this means that the nominees of the two major parties must be chosen in primary elections in the spring of general election years.

The majority of Texas cities and a variety of other units of local government such as school boards, on the other hand, have nonpartisan elections. That is, parties do not nominate candidates, and no candidate running for office can use a party label in his or her campaign. Candidates for office in such elections are self-nominated.

The Election Calendar

State law allows for general elections only on selected days. The vast majority must be held either on the third Saturday in January, the first Saturday in April, the second Saturday in August, or the first Tuesday after the first Monday in November. Elections for statewide offices, county offices, and national government offices are always held on the last of these dates. Many Texas cities elect their mayors and council members on this date, too, although a sizable number have their elections in April.

The Right to Vote

Virtually every U.S. citizen eighteen years of age or older who is a Texas resident is eligible to register to vote in the state. The only other exclusions are for those people judged mentally incompetent in a court proceeding; persons imprisoned or on parole or probation for a felony criminal conviction; and those who have been out of prison or released from probation for a felon conviction for less than five years.

Two active, if modest steps must be taken by those individuals who meet the preceding qualifications. They must first register to vote, which requires completing a simple, postage-paid form and mailing it to the Registrar of Voters in their home county. Then they must show up at the polls on election day. As we will explain, a large number of otherwise eligible Texans do not bother to complete these steps.

The Election Campaign

State law limits the timing and character of the election campaign. It does so, first, by setting the dates for primary and general elections and the procedures candidates and parties must follow to participate. State law also imposes a number of campaign finance requirements on candidates, parties, and, to a lesser degree, campaign contributors. In the latter instance, as an example, business corporations and labor unions are prohibited from making direct contributions to political campaigns. (They can, however, establish political action committees, or PACs, which can make contributions, as we will describe.)

The Texas Electorate

As aleady explained, there are several reasons why some people cannot or will not fulfill their civic duty by voting in elections. Some are precluded from doing so by state law, and some simply choose not to do so. We can describe the active Texas electorate, and the nonvoting population as well, by calculating the effects of these reasons for nonvoting in the 1990 general election in Texas. The reader may recall that in 1990 there was a spirited contest for the governorship between Ann Richards and Clayton Williams, and there were noted campaign battles for a number of other statewide, state legislative, congressional, and city government positions. It would appear, then, that the 1990 election could have produced a sizable turnout of voters simply because of the vigor of those election contests.

In 1990 there were 12,150,671 Texans of voting age, according to the U.S. Bureau of the Census. The Census Bureau's estimate, based on the decennial 1990 census, is probably a little low because of difficulties in implementing the census successfully. Yet that fact is itself offset by the hard-to-estimate number of felons and mentally incompetents among the voting age population who are not eligible to vote. Thus the Census Bureau's estimate is a good one for the eligible voter pool.

In the 1990 gubernatorial election 3,892,777 Texans actually cast ballots. Thus 32 percent of the voting age population participated in the election, a turnout rate that approximates that for all recent gubernatorial elections. Obviously, 32 percent voting participation is not very impressive, and such low turnout raises doubts about how democratic Texas politics really is.

Voting Turnout in Different Kinds of Elections

Voting turnout is affected to a remarkable degree by the nature of the election contest. Those elections every four years that feature a U.S. presidential race draw the highest voter participation. So-called "off-year" elections like those in 1990, when there is not a presidential race, produce the second-highest turnout. Municipal elections held at other dates, primary elections, and special elections on odd dates draw considerably fewer eligible voters to the polls.

We can illustrate these differences in the "drawing power" of elections by way of a few representative examples. In the 1988 election that featured the presidential race between George Bush and Michael Dukakis, 44 percent of voting age Texans voted, compared to the national average of 50 percent. In the 1990 off-year election, as noted above, only 32 percent of voting age Texans voted. In local elections to elect mayors and city council members, which are held separately from the presidential and off-year elections, it is not unusual for turnout to be as low as 8–10 percent of the voting-age population.

Obviously, voter participation in Texas elections does not indicate a healthy, vigorous democratic process. At best, less than half of the eligible electorate is making these decisions for the state. At worst, many local government elections are decided by a tiny fraction of the adult citizenry.

Money in Elections

Running for public office today can be very expensive. Campaigns for state offices like the governorship, state legislative seats, and local government positions in large metropolitan areas are especially costly. In all these races (save legislative seats in rural areas), candidates must rely on expensive mass marketing techniques like television, radio, and billboard advertising. One must spend a lot of money to get his or her message to a large number of far-flung voters.

In the 1990 governor's election, as the most expensive example, all the candidates combined were estimated to have spent $47 million. The two candidates who made it to the general election, Ann Richards and Clayton Williams, together spent about $36 million. Clayton Williams even spent over $8 million of his own money in his losing effort.

Other races are far less expensive but still remarkably costly. A competitive race for a state legislative seat can easily cost each candidate between $100,000 and $200,000. Many big-city mayoral and county government elections cost this much or more. Small-town and rural election races can be considerably less expensive, but a candidate may still have to spend several thousand dollars in the least expensive campaigns.

And where does this big money come from? A remarkable amount of it comes from special-interest groups and especially from their PACs—political action committees. PACs are organizations formed by interest groups, in accordance with state and federal law, to funnel campaign contributions to candidates who might support their causes. In most election races today, the bulk of a candidate's campaign contributions will come from PACs. The 1990 election races for the Texas Legislature offer good examples. One study showed that chairpersons of legislative committees—the most influential members of the legislature—received over 60 percent of all the contributions to their reelection fund from PACs. Some of these individuals got over 90 percent of their funds from PACs!

And which groups have PACs? Hundreds of different interest groups, from the rich and powerful to the small and not-so-wealthy, have these organizations and attempt to influence candidates with their contributions. Of most interest, however, are the big-spending PACs. Table 6.1 lists the ten biggest-spending Texas PACs in the 1990 elections. Not surprisingly, professional groups and business interests that are heavily regulated by the state, or whose profits are heavily influenced by state laws, are included in this group.

These figures on PAC spending are hardly comforting. With

TABLE 6.1   Texas's Biggest-Spending PACs in the 1990 Election

1.	LIFT (Trial lawyers)	$1,056,947
2.	TEXPAC (Physicians)	1,028,502
3.	TREPAC (Realtors)	629,981
4.	Good Government Fund (Bass family of Ft. Worth)	629,445
5.	Good Government Fund (Vinson & Elkins law firm)	528,112
6.	TEXDEN (Dentists)	440,883
7.	Texas Society of CPAs (Accountants)	380,317
8.	TSTA (Teachers)	283,579
9.	Texas Utilities	281,805
10.	NCNB Bank	274,045

Source: *The Houston Post,* March 4, 1991, A9.

low voter turnout on the one hand and with candidates for office remarkably dependent on special-interest money on the other, it is difficult to be positive about the health of democratic government in Texas. The rituals, forms, and procedures of democracy are observed at every election. But is this only show instead of substance?

Summary

1. Elections are the principal means by which the general public can collectively influence Texas governments.

2. The election process, including the participation of both political parties and individual citizens, is closely regulated by state law.

3. State law imposes relatively low hurdles for citizen participation in elections. Nonetheless, only small percentages of Texans vote in most elections.

4. Election campaigns are costly affairs and, perhaps unfortunately, candidates depend heavily on special-interest groups for their campaign funds.

5. The combination of low voter turnout and heavy reliance of candidates on special-interest groups to finance their campaigns should make us especially skeptical of the extent of public control of government in Texas.

7

The State Legislature

The legislature is, of course, the principal lawmaking body of state government. The governor and even the courts share some of the lawmaking power, but the legislature is the most important institution in this process. And the legislature is intended to be the principal means of achieving democratic control of government. The individuals serving in that body are supposed to follow the preferences of those who elected them to the office. How well they do so, however, is affected by who serves in the legislature and the circumstances under which they carry out their work.

Who Can Serve in the Legislature?

The Texas Legislature is composed of two houses, the Senate with thirty-one members and the House of Representatives with one hundred fifty. Each senator and representative is elected from a geographically specified district. In accordance with the requirements of the U.S. Constitution, these districts are redrawn every ten years after the U.S. Census so that all senators and representatives represent approximately equal numbers of

Texans. This redistricting requirement was imposed by the U.S. Supreme Court's "one person, one vote" decisions in the 1960s, in which the Court ruled that state legislative districts of unequal population sizes unconstitutionally diluted the representation of the residents of the larger districts. As a remedy, the court mandated regular, equal-population redistricting.

The Texas Constitution, on the other hand, prescribes the legal qualifications for members of these bodies. To serve in the house, one must be at least twenty-one years old, a citizen of the United States, a resident of the state for at least two years, and a resident of the district one would represent for at least one year prior to election. The requirements to serve in the senate are nearly identical except that one must be at least twenty-six years old and have been a resident of the state for at least five years.

These legal requirements, however, are not the most important ones that determine the membership of the legislature. Practical matters relating to the nature and demands of the legislator's job are more critical. Consider the nature of that job by way of explanation. First, one must get elected. And this process requires that the would-be politico enter the primary election campaign of one of the two major parties, raise a good deal of money for the campaign, spend the better part of his or her personal time campaigning, succeed in the primary election or the run-off election, and then continue the campaign against one's opponent from the other major party until the November election—and prevail in the latter contest. Simply getting elected, then, requires the better part of a year of one's time, effort, and money—and a good deal of other people's money, too, as Chapter 5 explained.

Once elected in November, the legislator has the immediate task of preparing for the regular legislative session the following January. That preparation requires several trips to Austin to be briefed by legislative leaders on the issues for the session and on the process by which the institution carries on its business. Then in January the legislator must effectively move to Austin until the end of May, when the 140-day regular session ends. Of course, not all the business of the legislature may be resolved in the regular session, and the members may be called back for one or more months or special sessions in the summer. For that matter, special sessions can be called at any time between regular sessions.

Regular sessions only occur once every two years, in odd-numbered years. Yet between these sessions, the work of the ambitious legislator must continue. He or she may have to work on one or more "interim" committees that carry out research on policy questions between regular sessions. Many of those people who elected the legislator will also be lobbying with regard to their public policy interests when the legislature is not in session. And the conscientious legislator would want to keep abreast of the interests and concerns of his or her constituents during this period.

In sum, the job is a demanding one. And those legislators who take it especially seriously, either because they are particularly concerned for the interests of their constituents or because they have strong personal interests in government policy, find it the most demanding. Yet for taking on this demanding job, legislators are paid the grand salary of $7,200 a year, plus $30 a day for living expenses when the legislature is in session.

The consequences of this situation are obvious. Only a fortunate few individuals can serve in the legislature. They must be independently wealthy or they must have occupations or business situations that allow them to be away from their jobs for long periods—while they are still earning the income from those jobs. And even such fortunate individuals will still consider their legislative career only a part-time job. Texas has, then, a part-time legislature made up of a very select group of citizens.

Who Does Serve?

Just what kind of people are these select citizens? The average Texas legislator is a white male in his mid-forties who has a law or other advanced degree and a business background. The legislature is about 90 percent male and 80 percent Anglo. More important, the vast majority of its members are from law, real estate, insurance, and a variety of other business and professional fields. Further, they have been sufficiently successful to overcome the practical and financial costs of membership described above.

What Do Legislators Do?

In Regular Sessions

When the legislature convenes for regular sessions in odd-numbered years, the principal work of considering new legislative proposals is delegated to the standing committees of each house. These are committees of legislators charged with reviewing proposed legislation in particular subject-matter areas. Members are assigned to these committees, principally based on the preferences of the presiding officers (the Lieutenant Governor in the Senate and the Speaker in the House), at the beginning of each regular session.

The early part of the regular session is largely devoted to committee review of new legislation, and the task is a formidable one. In recent regular sessions legislators have typically introduced about four thousand new bills and resolutions which must be considered for adoption. The committees must give all these various proposals an initial review, hold public hearings on many of them to hear the views of interest groups, government agencies, and individual citizens, and then decide whether to approve, reject, or revise and approve each bill.

If a bill is approved by a committee, it will go to the full House or Senate for consideration. If successfully passed at the latter level, it must go through the same process in the second house. And if the second house revises the original bill, the first house must approve those revisions or they must be agreed to by a conference committee of members of both houses. Eventually, however, the full House and Senate must vote to approve the bill in the same form. Finally, the governor must approve the bill—or the legislature must override the governor's veto if he or she rejects it—for the bill to become law.

The preceding explanation of the legislative process is the simplified version. The reality of the legislative process is actually far more complicated, for two reasons. First, the legislature follows complicated parliamentary procedures that govern when and how legislation can be introduced, how votes must be taken in the committee and the full house, how a bill rejected in the committee can be revived by other members of the house, when and how a bill will be scheduled for debate by the entire house,

Committees of the Texas Legislature

Senate Committees

Administration	Intergovernmental Relations
Criminal Justice	Jurisprudence
Economic Development	Natural Resources
Education	Nominations
Finance	Redistricting
Health and Human Services	State Affairs

House Committees

Agriculture and Livestock	Judiciary
Appropriations	Labor and Employment
Business and Commerce	Liquor Regulations
Calendars	Local and Consent
Corrections	Calendars
County Affairs	Natural Resources
Criminal Jurisprudence	Public Education
Cultural and Historical	Public Health
Resources	Public Safety
Elections	Redistricting
Energy	Retirement and Aging
Environmental Affairs	Rules and Resolutions
Financial Institutions	Science and Technology
General Investigating	State Affairs
Government Organization	State, Federal, and
Higher Education	International Relations
House Administration	Transportation
Human Services	Urban Affairs
Insurance	Ways and Means
Judicial Affairs	

and on, and on. The diagram of the "Basic Steps in the Texas Legislative Process" indicates a few of the details of this complicated process, but not all the many rules which govern it.

In addition, the legislative process is complicated because of the politics behind the scenes of the basic parliamentary rules.

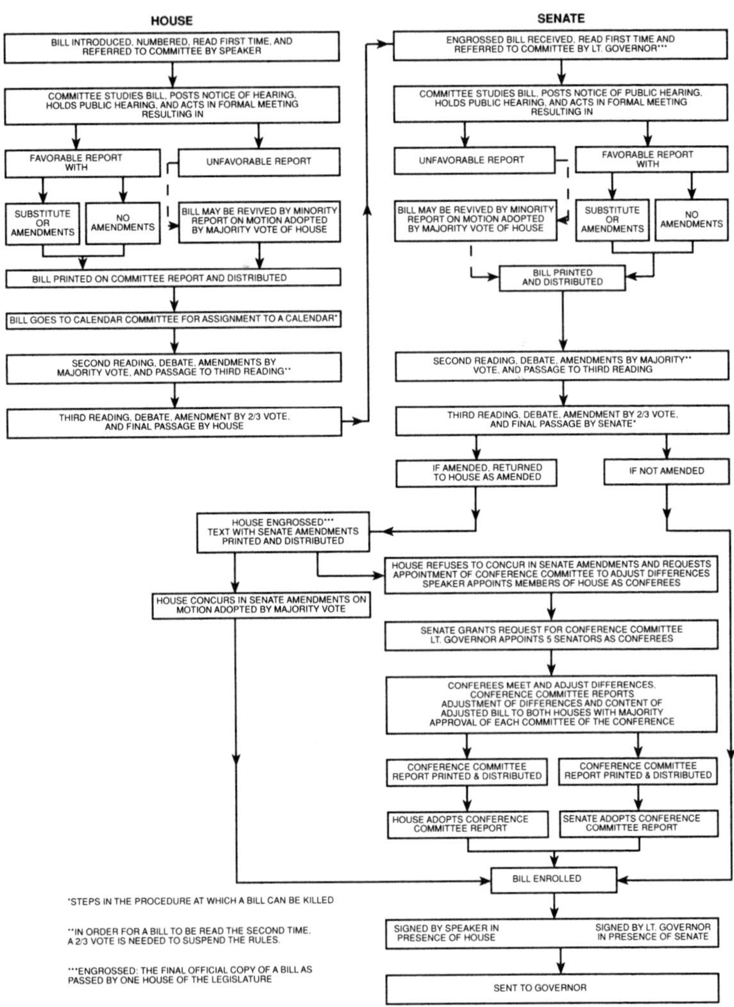

Basic Steps in the Texas Legislative Process

Source: *Texas Employment Commission.*

Chapter 7

Some members of the legislature are far more powerful than others, either because of their powerful supporters in interest groups and government agencies outside the body, their important committee leadership positions, or their associations with the Lieutenant Governor or the Speaker of the House. The latter two officials are so powerful themselves that they have been likened to feudal lords ruling their separate houses of the legislature like medieval fiefdoms. And the rules of the institution, along with the customary practices that grant great power to the Lieutenant Governor and Speaker, ensure that the legislature is hardly a democratic body itself. Powerful members can manipulate the rules of the game to a considerable degree to enhance their influence over the legislative process.

In Special Sessions

It has become more and more difficult for the legislature to fulfill all its important lawmaking obligations in the 140-day regular session. The agenda has grown dramatically in recent years, and some policy problems have been particularly vexing and time consuming. As a consequence, the legislature has frequently had to meet in special session to finish the agenda of the regular session or to grapple with problems too urgent to wait until the next regular session.

Special sessions are called by the governor, who also determines which topics the legislature may consider there. These sessions are limited by law to thirty days, but several can be called in succession if the legislature does not complete its work on the items put before it by the governor. What is most important about special sessions, however, is the pressure they place on lawmakers. These are brief, intense, highly conflictual meetings, with insufficient time for careful scrutiny of the legislation at issue. Thus as the state is governed increasingly by special sessions, it is more badly governed as well.

Between Sessions

As we indicated earlier, the work of the conscientious legislator does not end with the last day of the regular or special session. Policy problems and the needs of constituents deserve attention even when the legislature is not in session. And the members of the institution increasingly recognize this fact. One way they do so is by organizing "interim committees," which are special committees of legislators charged with investigating particular policy problems between regular sessions. In theory and sometimes in practice, interim committees can perform valuable research that will inform the decisions of the next regular session. But the utility of these committees is limited by the fact that few legislators can devote much time to them. After taking a "sabbatical" from their regular jobs during the legislative session, most legislators must restrict their attention to the government's business between sessions.

Summary

1. State law prescribes the minimum requirements for election to the Texas legislature. Practical matters, however, relating to one's income, occupation, and personal affairs are more important for determining who will serve there. Thus it is mostly select male, white businessmen who populate that body.

2. The legislature relies heavily on its standing committees and elaborate parliamentary rules to make its decisions. But behind-the-scenes politicking is a very important influence on those decisions as well.

3. The state constitution limits regular sessions of the legislature to 140 days' duration in odd-numbered years. But the increasing complexity of the legislature's work has meant that special sessions are almost always necessary to complete the work of the regular session.

4. Heavy reliance on special sessions means that the work of the legislature is being carried out less satisfactorily than we would desire. This is the case because special sessions are hurried affairs where insufficient time can be given to the study of policy problems and proposed solutions.

8

The Governor and the Executive Branch

Most Texans think the governor has a great deal of power —in the minds of many, the governor runs the state. Such expectations and assumptions about the governor's role and powers are not unreasonable. Certainly, chief executives are expected to develop the budget, appoint major administrators, and take the initiative in setting the public agenda. Executives are expected to be leaders. Yet the reality in Texas is far different from this expectation.

The Official Powers of the Governor

If the Texas governor succeeds in becoming an effective leader, it will be in spite of rather than because of the governor's formal and official powers. The state constitution simply does not provide the governor with a formidable array of tools. In fact, various studies have rated the Texas governor as the second weakest in the country in terms of formal power. In short, the deck is stacked against the state's chief executive. First, the constitution severely limits the governor's appointive powers, since, as we will discuss later in this chapter, many of the most powerful administrators in state government are elected rather than appointed. In fact, much of the executive authority and power that one would normally expect to find in the hands of the governor is given instead to these other elected officials.

The handful of positions that the governor can both appoint and remove are not very significant ones. In fact, none of these appointees are major policymakers. However, it would be wrong to assume that the governor makes few appointments. In fact, he or she fills several hundred positions in state government during the four-year term of office. By far, the most numerous appointments are to fill vacancies on the more than a hundred state boards and commissions, which we will discuss in more detail later. But even here the governor's powers are limited. First, members of these various boards and commissions serve six-year overlapping terms. One-third are filled every two years. The governor has to serve a full term before a majority of his or her appointees hold office. Second, the individuals selected to serve must often meet certain requirements that further limit the governor's discretion. For example, the appointee may have to be from a certain region of the state or be a member of a particular profession. Finally, the governor can't remove one of these officials from office.

The Texas governor is also very weak with respect to budgetary powers. The Legislative Budget Board (LBB), created in 1949 and dominated by the House and Senate leadership (the Speaker of the House and the Lieutenant Governor), actually writes the budget. The governor, however, has moderately strong veto power. For example, it takes a two-thirds vote of both houses to override a veto. The veto power is enhanced by the fact that many bills are passed by the legislature at the end of the session, making any veto final simply because the legislature has adjourned. Another factor that contributes to the veto power is the provision that gives the governor the authority to veto line items in appropriations bills.

The veto power is an exception to the pattern of gubernatorial weakness. When it comes to reorganizing and restructuring the bureaucracy, for example, the governor has little power. He or she has no authority to reorganize the administrative branch of government, and cannot consolidate individual agencies or bureaucratic functions, even if such steps were to eliminate duplication and waste and resulted in greater efficiency. This inability, along with the governor's limited appointive powers, virtually ensures that the governor exercises little real control over state agencies.

The pattern of limited formal power is further borne out by an examination of the governor's legislative powers. Many legislatures, including the national one, look to the chief executive to set the legislative agenda. The governor in many states is expected to propose a variety of new laws to deal with the state's problems, as the governor establishes priorities and provides leadership. Not in Texas. Instead, the legislature marches to the beat of its own drummer. But the governor does possess one significant legislative power that has been employed with increasing frequency in recent years. He or she can call special sessions of the legislature and set the agenda for it. This is an important power because it is essentially the only opportunity that the governor has to force the legislature to deal with policy issues of his or her choosing.

The "Unofficial" Powers of the Governor

If the Texas governor had no sources of power and influence at his or her disposal other than the ones specifically granted in the state constitution, few governors would leave a lasting imprint on the political life of the state. But there are other, informal sources of influence that the governor can rely upon, and if they are fully exploited, the governor's influence in the policy process can be dramatically enhanced. One major source of informal power flows from the governor's role as chief of state. Arguably, the lieutenant governor commands more formal power than the governor, and the Speaker of the House of Representatives may play a much greater role in the legislative process. But only the governor is the governor, and only the governor commands the same degree of attention and status. The prestige of the office is an asset of almost unlimited potential. Although the governor is unable to rely upon constitutional grants of power to establish budget priorities, he or she can, for example, call a press conference attended by representatives of

---

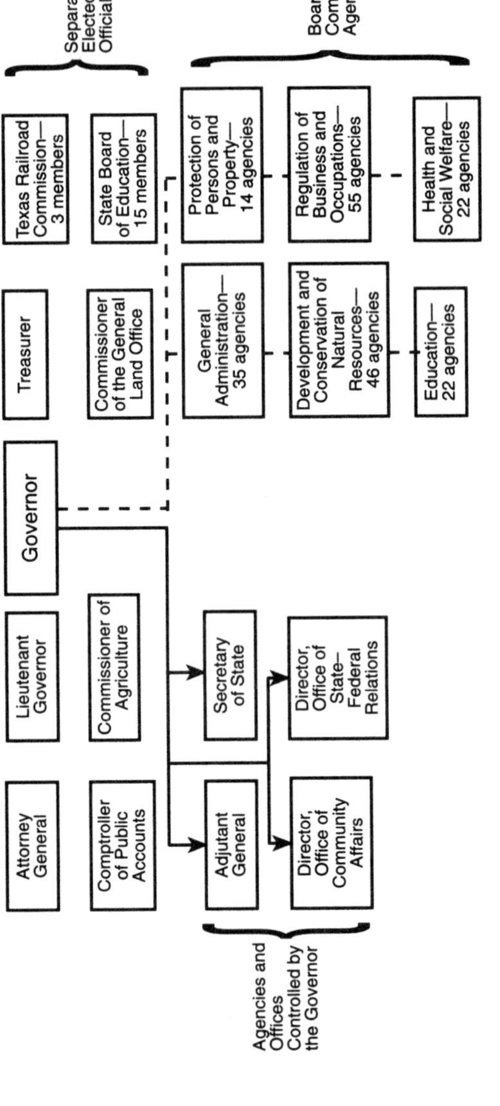

The Executive Branch of Texas State Government

major news organizations. That format can be exploited to call statewide attention to whatever issues the governor wishes to see addressed in the budget. The prestige of the office can be used to influence public opinion and, in turn, legislators. In a related vein, the average citizen believes that the governor is a powerful state official, and perception may well be as important as reality in this instance. People pay attention to what the governor says and are inclined to listen to his or her pronouncements. The governor's position on an issue can make a difference in public support or opposition and in the subsequent message that average citizens convey to their elected representatives.

The governor is also the head of the executive branch of government. Although his or her formal powers in this regard are limited, it is still the case that the governor sits directly astride a series of complex communications routes. Modern government is largely communications, within a network dependent upon the transmission, exchange, and processing of information. Knowledge translates into influence, and access to vast amounts of information, knowledge, and expertise is a potentially powerful tool that the governor can employ to achieve policy goals and political objectives.

Whether or not governors use the informal sources of power at their disposal is largely dependent upon their willingness to do so, which in turn is a function of personality. Some governors are "shrinking violets" who don't relish the exercise of power and do nothing more than what the job description requires—which, according to the state constitution, is precious little. They simply aren't interested in expanding the frontiers of gubernatorial power, and they allow the legislative leaders and other elected executive officials to run the state during their tenure in office. One wonders, given their passive style and apparent distaste for the passions of politics, why they sought political office in the first place. Perhaps they took office with every intention of becoming effective leaders but were intimidated by the governor's lack of formal power. In any event, this portrait of the passive, or at best mildly active chief executive, appears to be the norm in the state's political history. But there have been notable exceptions. One that readily comes to mind is John Connally, who served as governor in the 1960s. Articulate and outgoing, he was an ardent supporter of better public and higher education in the state. In recent years, governors have played an increasingly active role in pushing their policy agenda. For example, Mark White vigorously spoke out on behalf of educational reform in the public schools, while Bill Clements was an active spokesman in support of crime-control legislation. Ann Richards has vigorously pursued the reform of state government.

Even the most active, energetic, and engaging governor, however, will face major obstacles. The state constitution places a formidable—if not insurmountable—array of obstacles along the path to effective political leadership and policy success. The odds are stacked against the occupant of the governor's mansion. Public expectations are high, but formal powers and resources are low. As a result, the governor who can point to a substantial record of policy accomplishments as his or her legacy is rare indeed. So it is not surprising that the governor's office has seldom been used as a stepping-stone to positions of higher political calling. It is simply too difficult for even the gifted politician/executive/administrator to fashion a record of demonstrated accomplishment.

Recent Texas Governors

What types of Texans are elected governor? Typically, they have been middle-aged Anglo males who nominally, at least, are Democrats. In recent history, only one has been a Republican and only one (Ann Richards, the incumbent) a woman. They are typically college graduates and attorneys or wealthy businessmen. Most have had prior experience in government. John Connally, for example, was secretary of the navy in the Kennedy Administration. Mark White had served as attorney general, and Ann Richards had served as state treasurer.

The Executive Branch

When most people think of state and local government officials they think of governors, senators, representatives, mayors, and councilpersons. But there are only a few thousand of these elected officials in the entire state. The overwhelming majority of public officials—500,000 at the local level and 175,000 at the state level—are of a more mundane type. They include police officers, highway patrol officers, fire fighters, health and building inspectors, teachers, professors, animal control specialists, game wardens, prison guards, nurses, engineers, clerks, accountants, sanitation workers, economists, scientists, and medical doctors. Most of the day-to-day work of government is done by these several hundred thousand specialists. Their job is fundamentally different from that of elected officials.

Elected officials make the laws. Bureaucrats implement and enforce them. Elected officials emphasize responsiveness, promising something in return for the vote. Once elected, they play favorites by pursuing selected programs and policies that are more beneficial to some groups than to others. Bureaucrats, on the other hand, emphasize fairness rather than responsiveness. Rather than playing favorites by responding more favorably to some demands than to others, they attempt to be impartial by treating similar categories of demands equally. One of the reasons why citizens often feel frustrated as a result of their encounters with government revolves around this issue of responsiveness versus fairness. Government officials can't be responsive to the degree that citizens would like if they also try to be fair.

Bureaucrats are a powerful force in government because they control the delivery of services and the administration of programs. They are in charge of the machinery of government on a day-to-day basis and this fact gives them enormous influence. Another source of bureaucratic power is their experience and expertise. They are specialists in their particular area of operations, often devoting an entire career to working in the same department. Elected officials come and go, but bureaucrats are permanent fixtures who use their experience and specialized knowledge to overcome challenges to the way they run their agency. Discretion is another source of bureaucratic power. Sometimes the government employee *is* the service—the police officer on the beat, the teacher in the classroom, and the building inspector out on the job *are* the government services being provided. They enjoy enormous discretion. Some are conscientious and hardworking, while others are poorly prepared and little concerned with doing a good job. Some enforce the laws vigorously, consistently, and fairly, but others are capricious and arbitrary in their implementation of rules and regulations.

A final source of bureaucratic power flows from the bureaucrat's relationship with clientele groups. Administrative agencies were originally established to serve the public and to perform their job in the public interest. In practice, however, some interests are better served than others. Administrators develop relationships with those individuals and groups they most frequently interact with. For example, officials in an agency created to regulate the insurance industry or utility companies will, over time, find that their perspective and even their impartiality is influenced by the friendships and contacts they develop with industry representatives. These so-called clientele groups, in turn, are often relied upon to support larger appropriations for the agency and to defend it from attacks and criticisms.

Types of Executive Branch Agencies

The State of Texas has a complicated administrative system. In fact, there are three distinct types of state agencies. The first type consists of appointed boards and commissions. There are more than a hundred of these boards and commissions whose members (generally numbering six to nine) serve six-year overlapping terms and supervise the activities of a particular state agency. They are appointed by the governor and confirmed by the senate. Only infrequently are the members career bureaucrats. Generally, they are private citizens selected by the governor on the basis of campaign support, political connections, or prominence in a particular field. These boards set policy in a variety of areas. For example, in higher education university boards of regents establish board policy for the state's public universities. Other boards set policy in the areas of health and hospitals (Mental Health and Retardation Board), natural resources (Water Development Board), professions (State Board of Medical Examiners), prisons (Board of Pardons and Paroles), utilities (Public Utility Commission), and business (State Board of Insurance).

A second type of agency in the state consists of those whose chief officials are appointed by the governor and operate under his or her direct control. None of these are particularly important policymaking agencies. They include the secretary of state (keeps election statistics), adjutant general (commands the National Guard), labor commissioner (records and publishes labor statistics), executive director, Department of Community Affairs (coordinates federal and state programs relevant to local governments), executive director, Governor's Commission for Women (recommends new policies), and director, Office of State–Federal Relations (monitors federal legislation and federal grant programs).

A third type of agency has an elected agency head. These officials head some of the most important agencies in the state. They include the attorney general, the comptroller of public accounts (a key figure in the appropriations process), the state treasurer (chief financial officer), and the commissioner of the General Land Office (supervises more than twenty million acres of state land). Another important elected agency is the Texas Railroad Commission. Originally created to regulate the railroads, it today has the important responsibility of regulating the oil and gas industry in the state, as well as the transportation industry, including trucking and railroads. The three railroad commissioners are elected in statewide elections.

The executive and bureaucratic structure at the state level reflects the needs, values, and culture of nineteenth-century Texas. Political power is fragmented, control is divided, coordination is minimal, and accountability is essentially nonexistent. The governor lacks the authority and resources necessary to develop budget priorities, fashion a policy agenda designed to address major statewide issues and problems, and ensure that appointed administrators are both responsive and accountable. The division of executive power among a number of major elected officials hopelessly fragments the governor's control over policy initiation, formulation, and implementation.

Summary

1. Various studies have rated the Texas governor as the second-weakest chief executive in the nation in terms of formal powers. In Texas, much of the executive power and

authority one would expect to find in the hands of the governor is given instead to other elected officials.

2. None of the officeholders that the governor can both appoint *and* remove is a major policymaker. The governor is also weak with respect to the budgetary power.

3. However, the governor has the potential to exert major influence on the policy process if he or she exploits available informal resources. These include the status and prestige of the office and control over information.

4. The sources of bureaucratic power include control over the delivery of services, bureaucratic experience and expertise, administrative discretion, and relationships with clientele groups.

5. Texas has three different types of state agencies. The first type consists of appointed boards and commissions, the second is composed of officials appointed by the governor and accountable to him or her, and the third has an elected agency head. The latter category includes the comptroller of public accounts, the state treasurer, the attorney general, and the Railroad Commission.

6. The executive and bureaucratic structure in the state reflects the needs and values of nineteenth-century Texas. Political power is fragmented and accountability is limited. The governor lacks adequate authority and resources. The fragmentation of executive authority severely limits the governor's control over the formulation and implementation of policy.

References

BEYLE, THAD L. 1982. "The Governor's Power of Organization," *State Government* 55, 3:79–87.

BEYLE, THAD L. AND ROBERT DALTON. 1981. "Appointment Power: Does It Belong to the Governor?" *State Government* 54, 1:2–13.

ELLING, RICHARD C. 1983. "State Bureaucracies." In Virginia Gray, Herbert Jacob, and Kenneth Vines (eds.). *Politics in the American States.* Boston: Little, Brown.

GANTT, FRED JR. 1973. *The Impact of the Texas Constitution on the Executive.* Houston: Institute for Urban Studies, University of Houston.

9

The Court System

The courts make up the third branch of state government. Most of the business of the courts amounts to the resolution of rather ordinary disputes between private citizens in the civil courts, or between the government and one or more citizens in the criminal courts. The overwhelming majority of all these disputes are of concern only to the parties immediately involved. Of course, those parties have considerable personal interest in the character of the court system and how well it functions.

Yet all Texans, even those not directly involved in legal cases, should be concerned with the workings of the courts. The governor and legislature may make the laws, but it is judges, district attorneys, lawyers, juries, and police officials who ensure that those laws are properly enforced. If criminals escape punishment, if the law is not enforced equally for all litigants, or if the legal process is slow and costly, all Texans suffer—the extent to which we live in a civil society is diminished, and lawlessness and inequity are encouraged.

In addition, some cases in the courts have considerable political and policy significance. At times the law on the books is ambiguous, or two laws on the books may be contradictory to each other. The courts have the power to resolve these controversies, making law when they do so. Furthermore, some court cases have unusually far-reaching implications. For example, when the Texas supreme court ruled in 1989 that the method of funding public schools was unconstitutional, it created a huge policy problem that state and local governments have still not resolved. Thus all Texans should be interested in how, and how well, our courts function.

Which Courts Do What?

The state court system is a hierarchy where higher courts have review powers over the decisions of lower ones. Each level of courts also has particular, legally defined responsibilities for different kinds of cases. Generally speaking, there are three levels of courts: *trial courts,* which hear cases the first time they enter the legal system; *intermediate appellate courts,* which hear first-time appeals of trial court decisions; and *supreme courts,* which hear selected appeals of decisions in intermediate appellate courts.

The chart on the "Court Structure of Texas" indicates the specific courts at each of these three levels in our state, and it summarizes their jurisdiction in terms of the kinds of cases they can hear. We should briefly elaborate on the work of each of these courts, however.

The "lowest" courts are the justice of the peace and municipal courts, which settle disputes over minor civil and criminal matters. Over 70 percent of justice of the peace court cases, for example, are for minor traffic violations. In addition, these courts handle minor theft and assault cases, public intoxication, minor debt and foreclosure proceedings, and "small claims" disputes where the monetary value at issue is $2,500 or less.

Municipal courts handle very similar cases. Almost 90 percent of their docket is composed of traffic and parking cases. In addition, municipal courts consider alleged violations of city ordinances concerning such matters as building codes, fire safety, zoning, public health, and sanitation. These matters might not seem particularly interesting or notable, but the quality of urban life is fundamentally affected by local government regulation of them.

County courts are also restricted to the handling of relatively minor cases, though ones of more consequence than those of the

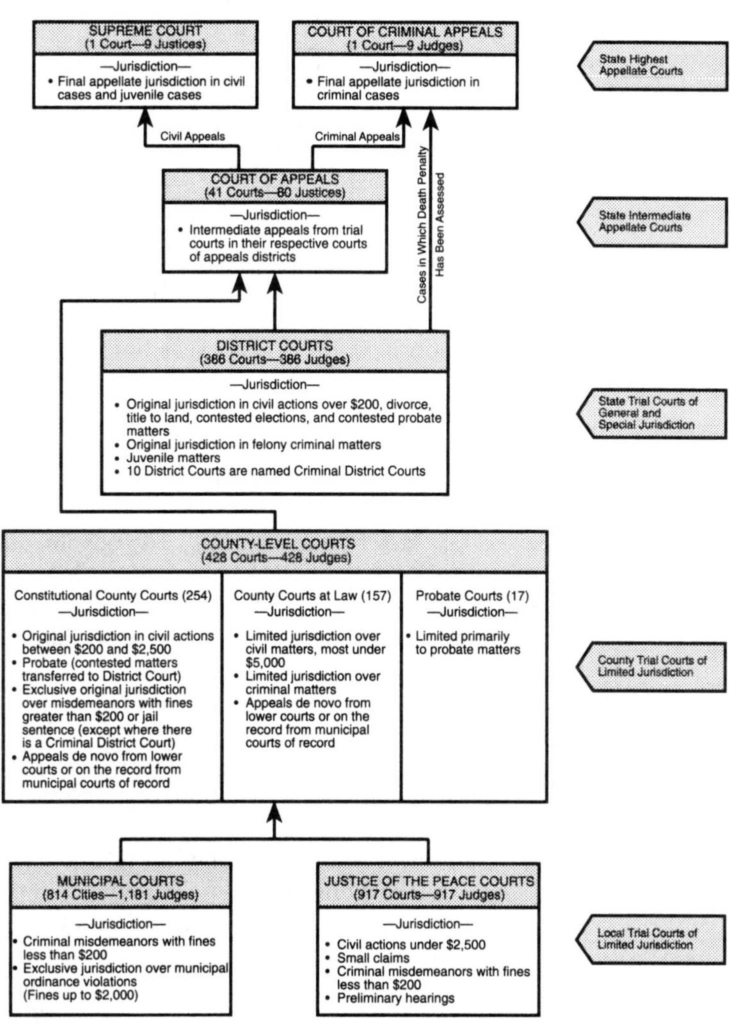

All Justice of the Peace Courts and most Municipal Courts are not courts of record. Appeals from these courts are by trial de novo in the county-level courts, or in some instances, the district courts. Some Municipal Courts are courts of record—Appeals from those courts are taken on the record to the county-level court.

Court Structure of Texas

Source: Office of Court Administration, State of Texas.

preceding two courts. In their criminal docket, county courts hear especially large numbers of driving while intoxicated, theft, and traffic cases. Their civil case load has especially large numbers of suits on debt, personal injury, probate, and mental health cases.

District courts are Texas's most important trial courts because they hear the most serious cases. Individuals charged with felony criminal offenses, for example, are tried here. The largest numbers of criminal cases, it should be added, are for charges of illegal drug sales or possession, burglary, theft, or assault. Yet criminal cases make up less than 30 percent of the caseload of district courts. Civil cases involving taxation, divorce, and other family matters are far more numerous than any of the individual categories of criminal offenses. Personal injury and debt disputes are quite common in these courts as well. The accompanying chart illustrates the typical mix of cases in the district courts.

Those individuals who lose cases in the district or county courts have the right to appeal the decision for a rehearing in the courts of appeals—if they can afford the additional legal expense of doing so. The latter courts do not hear new factual evidence or have juries to determine the outcome of the case. Instead, three-member panels of courts of appeals judges review the decision of the lower court to determine whether it followed the law and was free of procedural error. While these cases can be especially important because they may set precedents for future lower court decisions, only a very small percentage of lower court cases is ever appealed to this level. Less than 1 percent of all the cases settled in the district and county courts are appealed to the courts of appeals.

At the highest appeals level Texas actually has two courts—the supreme court, which is responsible for civil matters, and the court of criminal appeals, with responsibility for criminal cases. These courts hear appeals from decisions of the courts of appeals (with the exception that the court of criminal appeals hears death penalty appeals directly from the district courts). These two "supreme" courts have discretion, however, in which appeals they will consider. They have the power, that is, not to reconsider a case appealed to them, which means that the last lower court decision will stand.

Categories of New Cases Filed,
Year Ending August 31, 1990

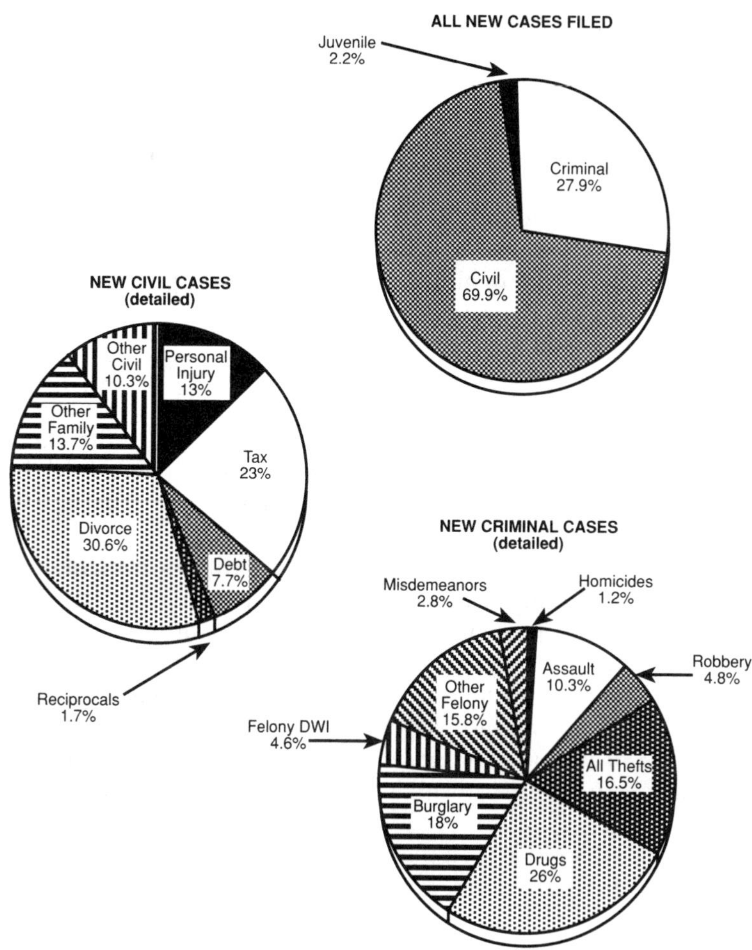

District Courts

Source: Office of Court Administration, Texas Judicial Council. *Annual Report, Fiscal Year 1990*. Austin, 1990, p. 164.

Officers of the Court

Judges

With the exception of those in municipal courts, Texas judges are publicly elected to their positions in partisan elections. They run for office, that is, as Democrats or Republicans, a fact which has been particularly controversial in the last few years. (Municipal judges are appointed by the local city government.) Critics of this partisan election system argue that it discourages many potentially good candidates from seeking judgeships and fails to focus attention on the most critical characteristics of those who do run—their legal qualifications. The critics argue for one or another system of appointing judges based on their technical legal competence.

Nonetheless, this partisan election system is called for by the state constitution, and any change in it would have to be made by a constitutional amendment approved by a majority of the state's voters. While such an amendment has not been put before the voters, they have been reluctant in the past to give up any of their election powers with other state offices.

To run for election as a judge in a district court or higher, one must be a licensed attorney and have spent a specified number of years in legal practice. Judges in constitutional county courts, justice of the peace courts, and municipal courts are not required by state law to be attorneys. Indeed the majority of the latter judges are not attorneys, although non-attorneys elected to justice of the peace positions, at least, are required to take a number of hours of college-level legal studies every year they are in office.

We should add as well that a large percentage of district and appeals court judges first get on the bench when the governor appoints them to fill a vacancy created by death or retirement. Because governors typically appoint loyal activists from their own political party to these positions, this is another way the composition of the bench is shaped by partisan politics.

Prosecuting Attorneys

County attorneys and district attorneys are also officials elected in partisan elections. They are the lawyers who prosecute individuals for the state in the county and district courts, respectively. District attorneys are especially important because they have considerable influence over grand juries, which must bring indictments for felony criminal offenses before an individual can be brought to trial. District attorneys also control the "plea bargaining" process whereby many criminal defendants agree to plea guilty in exchange for the lowering of the original charges against them.

Private Attorneys

While they are principally private businesspeople selling their services for a fee, attorneys are also members of a publicly regulated profession. They must be members of the state bar, an administrative agency of the judicial branch of government. The state bar and the supreme court regulate the practice of law in the state by prescribing the requirements for entering the legal profession and the ethical and legal standards for professional practice as an attorney.

The Jury System

The United States is virtually unique for its extensive use of the jury system, whereby average citizens are involved in the charging of individuals with crimes and in the determination of guilt or innocence in trials. Two different kinds of juries are involved here.

Grand Juries

These are panels of twelve citizens who serve three-to-six-month terms and who are responsible for determining whether the facts known to the police in particular cases warrant the charging of an individual with a felony criminal offense. District attorneys, as observed above, present these cases to the grand jury and advise it on the nature and strength of the evidence.

Trial or Petit Juries

These are the panels chosen to hear the evidence presented in court in particular cases and to determine guilt, innocence, and punishment in criminal cases; or to determine the settlement for the parties in conflict in civil cases. Trial by jury is a right guaranteed in the Texas and U.S. constitutions, but it can be waived by a criminal defendant or by mutual agreement of the parties to a civil suit. When that right is waived, the judge hears the evidence and determines the resolution of the case in what is then called a bench rather than a jury trial.

Summary

1. The court system of Texas is a hierarchy. The lowest courts hear minor legal cases. The district courts hear the most important ones, and the higher courts hear appeals of decisions from the lower ones.

2. Candidates for all but the lowest judicial positions must be lawyers. In the justice of the peace and county courts, however, where this professional status is not required, lawyers are in a small minority.

3. The activities of the court system are shaped by the work of several notable participants besides judges. Prosecuting attorneys represent the state and have particular influence over the outcomes of criminal cases. Private attorneys and citizens serving on juries also play key roles here.

10

Texans and the Law

The informed citizen should know more than the fundamentals of the court system as described in the preceding chapter. He or she should also have a basic understanding of the system of laws that are enforced by the court system, how those laws establish rights and obligations for Americans, and how disputes under these laws are resolved.

The Philosophy of American Law

American law is heavily, if not exclusively, rooted in English common law. Common law is not a system of fixed, precise laws made by legislatures or political executives. Instead it is based on the idea that there are "natural" or customary expectations for appropriate human relations. Thus the common law seeks to discover and follow those natural expectations.

There is a particular process, too, associated with the common-law tradition. Laws and their applicability to particular cases are "discovered" through an adversarial process where the parties involved argue their view of the case before a neutral, impartial "umpire," the judge. Either the judge or an impartial panel of everyday citizens, the jury, will then determine the outcome of the case. In effect, judges and juries determine how natural laws or customs should be applied to particular cases. Once a decision has been made in a common-law case, it becomes a precedent for future cases (the legal term for this use of precedent is *stare decisis*). Once a principle of common law has been discovered, in other words, it should be applied in the future to all similar cases. Thus in the common-law tradition, it is prior legal decisions and not formal codes of law set out by a legislature, as one alternative source, that guide legal decisions.

Both the philosophy and the practice of law are radically different in countries with other legal traditions. In the bulk of Europe, for example, the Roman legal system prevails. This system relies on a formal, rigid, written code of law established by a legislature or other official body. Thus judges do not need to "discover" the law, and they have little discretion in how it is applied. Instead, their role is to interrogate witnesses, establish the facts, and then apply the relevant code of law. Lay juries are seldom used in this system, as one other notable difference from the common-law system.

Kinds of Law

American laws arise from several different sources, and some sources are more important than others in the sense that they are "higher" forms of law. The common-law tradition is the source of a good deal of American law, so prior decisions of our courts applying common law principles are still relied upon in many legal cases. Over time, however, our governments have developed extensive legal codes much like those of the Roman system, and these codes also are the source of a good deal of our law. In effect, then, we have a mixed system of laws today, with some arising from common law and some from codified law. The most important sources of codified law are:

Constitutional Law

As described in Chapter 3, the highest law in Texas is that of the U.S. Constitution. The Texas constitution, also described in that chapter, is the second-highest source of law in the state. The provisions of the Texas constitution, it should be added, can pertain to matters not addressed in the U.S. Constitution, but they cannot conflict with the latter document.

Statutory Law

These are laws passed by the Texas legislature, and they cannot conflict with the provisions of the U.S. or Texas constitutions. Statutory law is important, of course, because constitutions only provide the general framework for the legal and governmental system, while statutes provide a good many of the myriad, specific details of law and policy. An example of a statute passed in 1989—in response to a controversy about sports agents recruiting Texas college athletes before they had completed their scholastic eligibility—is illustrated on the following page.

Administrative Rules and Regulations

This is an important category of law that is little understood by the average person. These are regulations made by state government executive branch agencies about how they will carry out their policy functions or how they will implement statutory laws whose enforcement the legislature has charged them with. Administrative regulations typically arise out of the following process: When the legislature passes a new law, it incorporates a number of the details of how the law should be implemented in the statute. But the legislature does not provide all those details or anticipate all the circumstances, special situations, or day-to-day aspects of implementing the law. Instead, the legislature grants to the relevant executive branch agency the power to write the administrative rules that will cover all those matters, with the stipulations that the latter rules must be in accordance with the intentions of the statute and that they be subject to subsequent review by the legislature.

Administrative regulations are more lengthy and detailed than the statutory laws for which they are written. Those rules are initially published in the semiweekly *Texas Register* and then compiled in the *Texas Administrative Code*.

S.B. No. 429

AN ACT

relating to the creation of the offense of soliciting, accepting, or agreeing to accept a benefit or offering, conferring, or agreeing to confer a benefit as an inducement to enroll in an institution of higher education and to participate in intercollegiate athletics; providing penalties.

Be it enacted by the Legislature of the State of Texas:

SECTION 1.   Subchapter D, Chapter 32, Penal Code, is amended by adding Section 32.441 to read as follows:

Sec. 32.441. ILLEGAL RECRUITMENT OF AN ATHLETE. (a) A person commits an offense if, without the consent of the governing body or a designee of the governing body of an institution of higher education, the person intentionally or knowingly solicits, accepts, or agrees to accept any benefit from another on an agreement or understanding that the benefit will influence the conduct of the person in enrolling in the institution and participating in intercollegiate athletics.

(b) A person commits an offense if he offers, confers, or agrees to confer any benefit the acceptance of which is an offense under Subsection (a) of this section.

(c) It is an exception to prosecution under this section that the person offering, conferring, or agreeing to confer a benefit and the person soliciting, accepting, or agreeing to accept a benefit are related within the second degree of consanguinity or affinity.

(d) It is an exception to prosecution under Subsection (a) of this section that, not later than the 60th day after the date the person accepted or agreed to accept a benefit, the person contacted a law enforcement agency and furnished testimony or evidence about the offense.

(e) An offense under Subsection (a) of this section is a Class A misdemeanor. An offense under Subsection (b) of this section is a felony of the third degree.

SECTION 2.   Chapter 13, Code of Criminal Procedure, is amended by adding Article 13.24 to read as follows:

Art. 13.24. ILLEGAL RECRUITMENT OF ATHLETES. An offense of illegal recruitment of an athlete may be prosecuted in any county in which the offense was committed or in the county in which is located the institution of higher education in which the athlete agreed to enroll or was influenced to enroll.

SECTION 3.   This Act takes effect September 1, 1989.

SECTION 4.   The importance of this legislation and the crowded condition of the calendars in both houses create an emergency and an imperative public necessity that the constitutional rule requiring bills to be read on three several days in each house be suspended, and this rule is hereby suspended.

Passed the Senate on March 6, 1989, by a viva-voce vote; passed the House on May 5, 1989, by a non-record vote.

Approved May 17, 1989.

Effective Sept. 1, 1989

Statutory Law on the Illegal Recruitment of an Athlete

City Ordinances

The state constitution allows cities with five thousand or more residents to adopt their own charter (as home rule cities) and write a number of their own laws as city ordinances. The scope of those ordinances, however, is restricted by both the state constitution and subsequent statutes passed by the legislature. City ordinances, which are compiled into a single volume called the city code, include regulations for the construction of residences and other buildings, residential subdivisions, traffic control, and the operations of a variety of businesses and occupations. In addition, the broad details of city services, such as those associated with airports, recreational facilities, utilities, and even cemeteries, are included. A copy of the city code is usually available to the public at city hall and at the city's public library.

Case Law

As explained in the preceding chapter, judges are often called upon to determine the applicability of statutes and other codified law to particular circumstances. They must also resolve many ambiguities and contradictions in constitutions, statutes, and administrative rules. Case law is the body of opinions of judges interpreting how the laws on the books should be interpreted or clarified in these ways. A portion of the body of case law also arises out of the common-law tradition.

Individual Rights Guaranteed by State Law

We are accustomed to thinking that the U.S. Constitution is the source of all individual rights and liberties, and it is the most important source of such guarantees. Yet state laws provide a number of additional individual rights. Some of the most noted of the latter provisions are in the Texas constitution, including those which stipulate that there will be:

> A guarantee of the right to vote in public elections as long as one is a citizen 18 years of age or older who is not an "idiot or lunatic," not a pauper supported by the county, and who has not been convicted of a felony.

Equality under the law regardless of one's gender [an "equal rights amendment" for women, which is not available in the U.S. Constitution].

No religious test for holding public office.

No *ex post facto* laws.

No "outlawing" of a citizen. That is, no "person shall be transported out of the State for any offense committed within the State."

"No conviction [for a crime] shall work corruption of blood or forfeiture of estate."

No imprisonment for debt.

No forced sale of one's homestead for debt except for that due on the purchase, taxes, or improvements on the homestead.

A good many individual rights are also established by statutory law and administrative regulations as well. An example of how administrative rules can establish such rights is provided by the statement of "Students' Rights and Responsibilities" from the 1989 *University Regulations* of Texas A&M University. That statement indicates certain fundamental guarantees this state agency makes its students, as well as certain expectations the university has for their behavior. The list of student responsibilities sounds like the University hopes for "apple pie and motherhood" behavior by students, but the rights assured students are substantial and important guarantees of just treatment.

Such legal rights can also be quite controversial. In 1991, for example, a group of Texas A&M faculty raised strong objections to including "sexual orientation" as a basis for equal treatment in the students' rights statement. Those faculty argued that no other state or federal laws guaranteed this right, and that some state laws even forbid certain homosexual acts. These objections were sufficiently strong that the university president struck this language from the statement of students' rights.

The Importance of Lawyers

The preceding discussion indicates that American law is a complicated subject. And those complications have importance

PREFACE

The following statement of students' rights and responsibilities is intended to reflect the philosophical base upon which *University Regulations* are built. This philosophy acknowledges the existence of both rights and responsibilities, which is inherent to an individual not only as a student at Texas A&M University but as a citizen of this country.

STUDENTS' RIGHTS

Article I
A student shall have the right to participate in a free exchange of ideas, and there shall be no University rule or regulation or administrative policy that in any way abridges the rights of freedom of speech, expression, petition and peaceful assembly as set forth in the U.S. Consititution.

Article II
Students shall be treated on an equal basis in all areas and activities of the University, regardless of race, color, religion, sex, sexual orientation, age, national origin or educationally unrelated handicaps.

Article III
A student has the right to personal privacy except as otherwise provided by law, and this will be observed by students and University authorities alike.

Article IV
Each student shall be free from disciplinary action by University officials for violations of civil and criminal law off campus, except when such a violation is determined also to be a violation of the provision regarding off-campus conduct in the Discipline Code of the *University Regulations.*

Article V
Each student subject to disciplinary action arising from violations of University regulations shall be assured procedural due process. At all judicial hearings, an accused student shall be assumed innocent until proven guilty, and, in initial judicial hearings, the burden of proof shall rest with those bringing the charges. In all proceedings, the student shall be guaranteed substantive and procedural due process.

STUDENTS' RESPONSIBILITIES

Article I
A student has the responsibility to respect the rights and property of others, including other students, the faculty and administration.

Article II
A student has the responsibility to be fully acquainted with the published *University Regulations* and to comply with them and the laws of the land.

Article III
A student has the responsibility to recognize that student actions reflect upon the individuals involved and upon the entire University community.

Article IV
A student has the responsibility to recognize the University's obligation to provide an environment for learning.

Students' Rights and Responsibilities

Source: Texas A&M University, *University Regulations*. College Station, May 1989.

for the average citizen. Imagine, for example, that you have a dispute with your landlord over your lease. What are your legal rights? What are your legal obligations? If the two of you cannot resolve this dispute amicably, where can you turn for help?

The legal system is your source of help, but it offers the same help to your landlord, too. But which part of the legal system will help ensure your rights? Because both the law and the court system are so complicated, we usually need the services of an attorney to resolve all but the most mundane of legal disputes. The attorney is our guide through the maze of the legal system. But we often need an attorney for a second reason as well. American law is based in part on an adversarial process, as noted previously. The parties to a legal dispute argue their case before the court as arbitor. And sometimes *how* and *how well* the case is presented determines the outcome, regardless of what the common law and the codified law say.

Even bargaining outside the courtroom has an adversarial character. A large percentage of civil suits is settled out of court based on bargaining between the two sides. Most criminal cases are settled out of court, too, by plea bargaining between the prosecuting attorney and the accused and his or her lawyer. (Over 90 percent of all criminal convictions in Texas courts are based on guilty pleas, and most of these arise out of plea bargaining.) Thus we frequently need an attorney as our advocate and professional negotiator. In any serious legal case we ideally need an attorney who is, first, thoroughly knowledgeable of the relevant law and of typical out-of-court bargains in similar cases. We also need someone who is clever, tough, and a "bulldog-mean" negotiator.

Legal Guidance for the Layperson

We may need an attorney when we are actually involved in a legal dispute, but few Texans can afford the advice of a lawyer every time they have a question about the law. And many of our everyday family and business affairs have important legal implications. Thus if we know some of the details of the law on such matters, we are far more likely to ensure our own legal rights and live up to our legal obligations.

Small Claims Courts—Where a Lawyer Is Not Required

There is one place in the court system where an individual can seek justice without having to hire an attorney—in a small claims court. These courts, which are simply Justice of the Peace courts acting under informal rules, allow individuals to file and argue their own legal case in layman's terminology.

If you have a dispute with another Texas resident in a matter involving $2,500 or less, you can file a small claims case to resolve the matter. You must file a statement (see the accompanying illustration) with the Justice of the Peace judge whose geographic jurisdiction includes the residence of the defendant or the place where the defendant contracted to perform a service or act that led to the dispute. You must also pay a modest filing fee, which you can recover if you win the case.

The judge then issues a citation for the defendant to appear, along with you, for a hearing. A small claims court hearing is informal with, according to the law, "the sole objective being to dispense speedy justice between the parties." You and the defendant can both present your side of the dispute to the judge in layman's terms. You can question the defendant, the defendant can question you, and you can bring other witnesses or have reluctant ones subpoenaed (for a fee). You can even have a jury trial if you request it.

If you win the case, the defendant must either pay the settlement or appeal the decision to the county courts, where the case will be retried also in the informal, small claims format. If the defendant fails to pay the settlement, the justice of the peace can help you pursue further legal action to gain your money.

We can learn some of these elementary details through commercially available books on law for the lay person. An old but still quite accurate discussion of the strengths and weaknesses of the Texas constitution is provided by

George D. Braden. 1972. *Citizen's Guide to the Texas Constitution.* Austin: Texas Advisory Commission on Intergovernmental Relations.

A Representative Small Claims Legal Statement

In the Small Claims Court of ____________ County, Texas

A.B., Plaintiff

C.D., Defendant

State of Texas

County of ____________

A.B., whose post office address is ________ (street and number), _________ (city), _________ (county) County, Texas, being duly sworn, on his oath deposes and says that C.D., whose post office address is _________ (street and number), _________ (city), __________ (county) County, Texas, is justly indebted to him in the sum of ____________ Dollars and ____________ Cents ($ __________) for ________________________________

____

____

____

(here the nature of the claim should be stated in concise form and without technicality, including all pertinent dates), and that there are no counter claims existing in favor of the defendant and against the plaintiff, except __________________________ (if any).

____

        Plaintiff

Subscribed and sworn to before me this ___ day of _____, 19___.

____

        Judge

By:

____

        Clerk

Guidance on general legal matters is provided by

> Ralph Walton and Charles Turner. *Texas Law in Layman's Language*. Houston: Gulf Publishing Co.

> Richard M. Alderman. *Know Your Rights! Answers to Texans' Everyday Legal Questions*. Houston: Gulf Publishing Co.

For legal advice on business affairs, a topic of wide interest, one can consult such works as

> Richard Alderman and Tom Oldham. *Your Texas Business*. Houston: Gulf Publishing Co.

> Anthony Mancuso. *How to Form Your Own Texas Corporation*. Berkeley, California: Nolo Press.

Summary

1. American law is a mixture of common law created by court decisions and codified law produced by legislatures and administrative agencies of government.

2. Various state laws provide for individual rights beyond those included in federal law.

3. The services of a good attorney are often critical to one's success in a legal controversy. Attorneys know the details of the law and of court procedure, both of which are quite complicated. A good attorney will be a tough negotiator, a critical factor in the best presentation of one's case.

4. Average citizens can learn about their legal rights and responsibilities by studying various guides to the law, and they can even represent themselves in small claims courts, getting justice without the expense of hiring an attorney.

11

Texas Cities

This chapter examines the characteristics, structures, and processes of city governments in the state and differences between municipal and state governments. It also analyzes the different forms of government in Texas cities, and the impact that these governments have on policy, as well as the changing nature of urban areas.

City and State Government Compared

There are some fundamental differences between city government and state government in Texas. These differences make it more difficult to govern a city than to govern the state. First, public services in the city are delivered daily and frequently involve an encounter with a public employee. The services delivered by the state government are generally less conspicuous. In addition, city services, such as police, fire, and education, are essential in nature. Because virtually every person depends on these services, they tend to be more concerned with their quality. Further, local government is more accessible to citizens than is state government. If citizens want to express their views, they can easily locate the appropriate local official, so they are more inclined to attempt to influence local government activities. There is also an element of bureaucratic discretion in local government. Often, the bureaucrat *is* the service—such as the teacher, police officer, or building inspector. The discretion given to these bureaucrats makes the job of local government officials more difficult. Citizens may also express different demands for the same local service. Because of these conflicting demands and expectations, it is often impossible for local government to satisfy all citizens. Finally, cities and states are influenced differently by other levels of government. For example, the federal government can intervene and force certain changes within city electoral structures, and county and state jurisdictions can also limit the power of a city. The state may dictate tax levels and types for a city.

These characteristics complicate policymaking at the local level. The services that city governments provide are essential to the citizen's health, safety, and well-being. If citizens perceive that these vital services are not being provided at an adequate level, they are likely to demand that local public officials do something to improve the situation. However, different groups of citizens sometimes demand that government do different things about the same service. And the physical closeness of local public officials makes it much easier for citizens to complain about unsatisfactory service levels. In addition, city governments often lack the power and resources to solve many problems, since their authority is limited by both the state and federal governments. Therefore, they cannot adequately respond to citizen demands for action.

Forms of City Government

The different forms of municipal government in Texas derive their structure from the two basic traditions in city government—reformed and unreformed. The three forms of municipal government are

- The mayor–council system
- The manager–council form
- The commission.

Each of these forms of government was created at a particular time in American history in response to the particular problems of the period. We can understand the character of these different kinds of government and why they were created if we consider a little of that history.

The U.S. Constitution reflects the agrarian society that existed when it was written. It mentions the national government, the state government, and the people, with no reference to cities. Therefore, cities are creations of their state governments. Municipal government became increasingly important with the onset of industrialization, as the need for labor resulted in a concentration of Eastern and Southern European ethnic groups within the cities. The new form of local government that arose in response to the needs of working-class ethnic Americans was the urban political machine. This machine had the following characteristics

- Popularly elected mayor with official power
- Power sharing with unelected machine bosses
- Highly responsive to its constituents
- Emphasis on a web of mutual obligations between voters and public officials. Some claimed that the machine led to favoritism, inefficiency, and corruption.

Although the political machine is virtually nonexistent today, those cities with some characteristics of that type of government are known as unreformed cities. Unreformed governments have the following characteristics:

- A strong mayor, elected by popular vote, who has executive and administrative authority
- A city council selected from wards that provides for ethnic, racial, and income group representation
- Political parties that contest elections, and candidates who are identified on the ballot according to party affiliation (partisanship)
- Jobs in municipal government that are filled by patronage (spoils system).

The corruption and ethnic control of the urban political machine led to what historians refer to as the reform movement. Reformers wanted to remove politics and conflict from city government so that municipal officials could concentrate on the essential tasks of running a city. The reformers emphasized efficiency, effectiveness, and the "public interest" over favoritism, responsiveness, and strictly local interests. This movement toward neutral professional competence in the executive branch proved successful in many Texas cities. These so-called reform governments have the following characteristics:

- An appointed city manager has executive and administrative authority
- A city council is responsible for policymaking and the manager is expected to carry out the policy
- Nonpartisan elections
- Each member of the city council is elected at-large by the entire electorate
- City employees are hired on the basis of merit, not patronage.

The intent of the reformers was to run the city as a business, according to principles of scientific management. Their model was the business corporation with its stockholders, board of directors, and chief executive officer. Their belief was that the primary function of the city was to perform housekeeping tasks (repairing and cleaning the streets, providing police and fire protection). Consequently, they saw no need for political parties and political conflict. Today, most large Texas cities have reformed governments. However, some exhibit characteristics generally associated with unreformed structures. For example, Houston has a strong mayor system and both Houston and Dallas elect many council members from wards.

The commission is another form of city government. It was first used in Galveston in response to the aftermath of a killer hurricane in 1900. This form places legislative, executive, and administrative responsibilities into the hands of several elected commissioners. Each of these commissioners also serves as the head of a major department. As a body, they act as the city council. Although popular in the first part of the century, the commission is a little-used form of city government today.

Municipalities may be further classified as general-law or home-rule cities. General-law cities operate under a uniform set of laws and restrictions set by the state government and are more likely to use the mayor–council form of government. Cities must have a population of over five thousand to adopt their own charters and become home-rule cities.

Participation in Urban Areas

Voting is one of the most widespread forms of political participation, but local and municipal elections attract relatively few voters. In fact, in no Texas city does the election of mayor attract more than 35 percent of the registered voters. Bond elections, in which voters decide on methods of financing for city improvements, attract even fewer voters. In addition, the number of registered voters is far less than the number of those eligible to vote by age, making voter turnout even lower. There are several reasons for low voter turnout. State elections draw more voters because they are perceived as more important than local elections, electing more prominent officials and getting more media coverage. In addition, the involvement of political parties in state elections raises the level of voter turnout. Special-interest groups also tend to be more involved in state elections. Accordingly, these groups encourage their members, as well as other citizens, to vote for the candidates they support.

Conservative voters tend to dominate the local electorate because lower-income voters are less likely to participate. Political participation is generally class biased in that those who participate tend to be of higher income, education, and social status than those who do not participate. The absence of political parties also results in fewer low-income voters participating in local elections. Consequently, public policy tends to be conservative because government officials respond to those who actively participate.

Citizens can also affect local government by participating in interest groups. In local government, these groups are often made up of citizens with neighborhood concerns. They typically work to protect and improve their neighborhoods, and they serve as "watchdogs" for the interests of the community. Groups that represent business interests are often the most effective political organizations at the local level, as their resources can provide financial support for candidates. Business groups also enjoy status and legitimacy that enable them to have special relationships with candidates and public officials. Since business interests are associated with economic growth, they often share common goals with local leaders.

The structure of interest groups in Texas cities has changed over the past twenty-five years. Urban politics in Texas is no longer dominated by a small, powerful group of white bankers, developers, oil barons, and politicians. Although the business community remains influential in local affairs, it now exercises that influence in an environment where power is shared with many other groups. These groups include blacks, Hispanics, women, gays, environmentalists, and neighborhood organizations. The Texas city is a much more open and democratic political arena today than it was twenty-five years ago.

Race and the City

Houston is now a nonwhite city. Only 37 percent of Houston's population is white, while 31 percent is black, 27 percent is Hispanic, and 5 percent is Asian. And Houston is not alone. Virtually every major Texas city today has a nonwhite majority. As the large cities in Texas become both poorer and more heavily populated by minorities, the suburbs surrounding them remain white and wealthy.

Race and poverty are closely connected. Between 1980 and 1990, the Hispanic poverty rate in Houston rose from 19 percent to 30 percent, while Hispanic family income fell to $19,000 from $25,281. Dallas Hispanics also have a 30 percent poverty level. In El Paso, more than 60,000 people live in the slums known as colonias, which lack even running water and sewer systems. This environment of poverty tends to crush the expectation that education will make things better. In Houston, 54 percent of all Hispanic students currently enrolled in the seventh grade are expected to drop out before they graduate. The corresponding figure for black students is 48 percent.

Suburbanization

As the central cities in the state have become older, poorer, and more nonwhite, white and wealthier Texans have moved to the suburbs in huge numbers. Part of the reason for doing so can be attributed to race. Many whites don't want to live in central-city neighborhoods surrounded by ever-increasing numbers of blacks and Hispanics. By moving to the suburbs, the white citizen can still work in the central city but live in an essentially all-white suburb.

But race is not the only factor in accounting for suburban flight. The schools are also a major consideration. Many families believe that their children can get a much better—and safer—education in the suburbs. Crime is also a factor. Central cities are seen as much more dangerous than the suburbs. The city is perceived as a place of social disorganization and decay, characterized by high crime and high taxes. Drug use is rampant, the schools are atrocious, and public services are inadequate. On the other hand, the suburbs are seen as a place where traditional "family" values are still dominant. In the suburbs one finds few minorities, few poor people, stable and even increasing property values, efficient government, good schools, and superior service levels. The suburbs attract, while the city repels.

The central city finds itself confronted with an extremely difficult situation. Needs increase and revenues decline. If taxes are raised in response to increasing needs and declining revenues, more people and businesses will exit the city and further erode the deteriorating tax base. The difficulties of the central city are compounded by the fact that the state provides the cities with little financial help, even as federal aid has steadily declined over the past several years.

Three elements dominate the city—land, labor, and capital. The city controls only the land. Labor (people) and capital (money and technology) are free to move anywhere within the fragmented urban area. The city is primarily concerned with stimulating economic growth because growth creates jobs and enhances the revenue base. A high revenue base provides bigger budgets and keeps taxes low. Citizens with jobs pay taxes and make fewer demands upon the government for expensive social welfare programs and services. In order to attract new business and stimulate economic development, the city seeks to provide good public services—education, police and fire protection, recreation, transportation, and low taxes.

The city has little incentive to take care of the poor and disadvantaged. Social welfare programs cost money and add little to the revenue base, and don't attract new businesses or create new jobs. The city has much more interest in building additional freeways, modernizing the airport, constructing a new sports arena, adding a convention center, rebuilding the water and sewer system, and hiring more policemen and firemen. These developmental activities enhance the economic attractiveness of the city, stimulate growth, and create new jobs. Public welfare and housing programs do not.

Despite the efforts of public officials and groups in the central city to stem the tide of white flight to the suburbs, their efforts have not been particularly successful. Increasingly, the huge cities in Texas are poor and nonwhite. Some of the most severe social and economic problems Texans will experience in the next several decades will be disproportionately concentrated in the cities.

Summary

1. The major forms of city government in Texas are the mayor–council system, the manager–council system, and the commission.

2. The mayor–council system places executive and administrative power in the hands of an elected mayor, while in the manager–council city the chief executive official is a professional manager appointed by the council.

3. Major forms of participation in urban areas in the state in-

clude voting, contacting a public official, interest-group activity, nonviolent protest, and exiting the city for the suburbs.

4. Political participation is class biased in that those who participate tend to be of higher income and education. The local electorate is dominated by conservative voters, and local government officials respond to those who actively participate.

5. Texas cities are much more open and democratic political environments than they were twenty-five years ago. However, as the central cities in the state have become poorer and increasingly nonwhite, Anglos have moved to the suburbs in huge numbers.

6. The difficulties of the central cities—loss of jobs and wealthy citizens and declining revenues—are compounded by the fact that the state government provides them with little help. Also, federal aid has steadily declined in recent years.

12

Other Local Governments: Schools, Counties, and Special Districts

Texans are served by a variety of local governments besides cities, and the most important of these are school districts, counties, and so-called special districts. Each of these kinds of governments provides particular services, and each kind has distinctive problems. Our survey of Texas government would not be complete without some attention to these matters.

School Districts

There are more than a thousand school districts in Texas. Each district is governed by a school board or board of trustees elected by the voters of the district in a nonpartisan election. The school boards' duties include appointing a superintendent, hiring teachers, selecting textbooks, setting the property tax rate in the district, approving the budget, controlling the construction of district buildings, and establishing broad policy for the school district. The State Board of Education sets general educational policy and the Texas Education Agency implements it. Financing for public schools is provided for by both the state and the local school district.

Should the sins of the father be visited on the children? In Texas, where many believe poverty is a sin, or at least a condition visited upon the undeserving, the answer is yes. This is certainly the case for public school expenditures. In the 1990–1991 school year, the wealthiest school district in the state—Laureles—spent $33,600 per student. The poorest district—Edcouch Elsa—spent only $3,485. Amazingly, however, Edcouch Elsa has a property tax rate that is almost three times as high as Laureles ($0.93 per $100 of property versus $0.35 per $100 in Laureles). It makes no difference. The far greater wealth in the Laureles district ensures that it can spend $30,000 more on each student.

These disparities in property wealth exist across the entire state, not just at the extremes. Of the more than a thousand school districts in the state, more than two-thirds have taxable property wealth below the state average of $22,000 per student. The average taxable property value in the poor districts is only about one-fifth that of rich districts. These disparities in prop-

TABLE 12.1 Texas Public School Districts by Number of Students

Total Number of Students	*Number of School Districts*
Less than 100	66
100 to 249	135
250 to 499	185
500 to 999	216
1,000 to 2,499	243
2,500 to 4,999	119
5,000 to 9,999	70
10,000 to 24,999	48
25,000 to 49,999	23
50,000 or more	8

Source: U.S. Bureau of the Census, *Census of Governments, 1987: Government Organization.* Washington, D.C., 1988, p. 28.

erty value are so great that even if the poor districts tax themselves at a higher rate they cannot catch up. However, the vast differences between educational expenditures in rich and poor districts will no longer be so great. The Texas Supreme Court recently upheld a lower court decision that found the state system of financing public education to be unconstitutional. Consequently, the legislature is scrambling to devise a funding scheme that will satisfy the court. These developments, which deserve careful attention, represent one of the most significant policy changes in the history of Texas politics and will exert a major impact on the educational system in the state.

The Texas Constitution of 1876 specified that education is "essential to the preservation of the liberties and the rights of the people." The constitution also established the Permanent School Fund, which drew its revenues from public lands in the state. The first payment to local schools from this fund was made in 1877 and was in the amount of $3.57 per pupil, calculated on a per-student basis. Yet inequities in expenditures across school districts were soon evident. Many town schools significantly augmented state aid with local tax revenues, while rural schools did not. The first effort at equalization came in 1915 when the legislature appropriated a million dollars for rural districts. In 1937, an equalization fund was established to make payments to districts with low levels of taxable property.

In 1949, the state created the Minimum Foundation Program, which provided for state funding of 80 percent of the cost of a school program based on a set of minimum services. School districts were then free to use local tax revenues to augment these expenditures. The wealthy ones did, while the poor ones could not afford to. A new version of the Foundation Program established in 1975 specified that state-aid formulas to local districts would be linked to actual property values in each district.

Attempts at equalization had little effect upon the widening gap between rich and poor districts. This can be attributed in large part to the fact that local tax revenues account for a significant share of educational expenditures. Public education in the state costs more than fifteen billion dollars a year. Of this amount 46 percent comes from local tax revenue and 39 percent from the state. The remainder is accounted for by federal aid and debt. Since the single largest share of school funding comes from local tax sources, it is easy to see why gross disparities in school district property values result in gross disparities in educational expenditures.

The first major challenge to the state's system of public school funding came in the form of a federal lawsuit. In 1971, Demetrio Rodriquez, a parent, filed a suit alleging that the school finance system was unconstitutional since it led to unequal outcomes (expenditures) that arose because of vastly unequal access to taxable property wealth. The federal district court judge agreed and held that the state method of funding public education violated the equal protection clause of the Fourteenth Amendment. Two years later, however, the United States Supreme Court would overturn *Rodriquez* v. *San Antonio Independent School District* and preserve the way Texas financed its public schools. In this decision, the Supreme Court ruled that, unlike the freedom of speech, press, religion, and assembly, education was not a fundamental right and consequently was not entitled to constitutional protection. The Court ignored the argument that a poor child's right to equal access to education greatly enhances the individual citizen's opportunity to effectively exercise the fundamental rights of speech, press, and assembly.

In any event, the old funding system remained essentially intact for almost two more decades. However, the legislature continued through 1990 to tinker with the various component parts in an effort to achieve some measure of equity. These efforts, however, were too little and too late. In 1987, state district Judge Harley Clark held in *Edgewood* v. *Kirby* that variations in educational expenditures based on unequal access to property wealth were constitutional. This decision was upheld by the Texas Supreme Court in 1989. Similarly, the efforts by the legislature in 1990 were also declared unconstitutional in 1991 by the Texas Supreme Court because they didn't go far enough toward resolving the equalization issue.

The state is now under court order to develop a plan to equalize expenditures for the public schools. The legislature is considering a variety of proposals, and the final outcome will probably incorporate some combination of tax-base consolidation and the shifting of state and local spending responsibilities. For example, in 1991, there existed a 585-to-1 disparity in property wealth between the richest and poorest school districts. One proposal would reduce this disparity to 7-to-1 by creating 204 school finance authorities along with county lines. Whatever specific program is eventually adopted, it is certain that the outcome will be a much more equitable system of school funding than has ever existed in the state's history.

Even though the equalization of expenditures represents a major step toward educational reform, Texas still fares poorly when compared with other states. Ironically, only one other state, Missouri, spends as great a share of their state and local budget on education as Texas (28.6 percent). Unfortunately, this does not translate into a favorable set of outcomes when Texas is compared with other states. Of the ten largest states, Texas has the largest percentage of school-age children and the largest percentage of those children living in poor households. The demands of a large and poor student population create a greater need for educational programs and services. However, Texas ranks last among the ten largest states in per capita educational spending. Similarly, Texas teachers were paid an average of $26,513 in 1989, while the national average was $29,567, ranking Texas thirty-first out of the fifty states.

Counties

The county form of government is strongest in rural areas and is generally limited in its responsiveness, efficiency, and effectiveness. In theory, the county is an administrative arm of the state established to collect taxes and carry out state laws and policies. In practice, the county is able to choose its course with respect to the services it provides or the property taxes it imposes, within the limits established by the state constitution and state law. The powers given to the county by the state constitution are not significant. However, the structure and function of the county government offices are specific. Since counties do not have the option of home rule, the smallest county is run just like the largest county. The county government structure reflects a form of government adopted to serve a rural state, and the constitution makes no provision for adaptation in response to changing conditions. An amendment to the state constitution adopted in 1933 provided for home rule, but its ambiguity led to

---

its deletion in 1969. However, the expansion of urban areas within so many Texas counties may lead to a demand that more problem-solving power be given to the counties. State law greatly limits the amount of authority that a county can have. Although some counties have increased their responsibilities, this growth can be attributed to federal funds and court orders that require counties to carry out certain responsibilities.

Officials of County Government

The Commissioner's Court

The commissioner's court is the closest thing to a central policymaking body in county government. Each court consists of four commissioners and a county judge. Each commissioner is elected from precincts of approximately equal population and is responsible for county road and bridge construction and maintenance in his or her respective precinct. Other responsibilities include:

- Setting service charges and fees
- Approving the county budget
- Appointing various county officials
- Filling vacancies in office
- Assigning contracts for supplies and equipment
- Drawing the boundaries for justice of the peace
- Deciding on which state programs will be adopted and funded
- Submitting proposals on special taxes to the voters.

The commissioner's court has the power to determine certain services and the tax rate, within state constitutional limits. It also decides upon various optional programs and facilities. However, the only tax it can levy is the property tax, which is essentially fixed by the state. In addition, the court's ability to influence how county dollars are spent is limited. The commissioner's court is also constrained by self-imposed limitations.

Traditionally, the court has not sought to expand its powers, to provide more services or programs beyond a minimal level, or to assume responsibility for addressing and resolving a variety of countywide problems. This allows the commissioners to concentrate on certain areas such as roads and bridges, while at the same time insulating them from public pressure for increased services.

The County Judge

The county judge is elected at-large by the county electorate and is responsible for the following:

- Preparing the county budget
- Posting election notices and forwarding election results to the state
- Serving as judge of the county court, which includes probate jurisdiction
- Issuing licenses for the sale of wine and beer in the county.

The structure of a county's judicial system results in few judicial responsibilities for county judges. However, the judge's informal duties as the county's dominant political leader may lead to resolving disputes about services and programs. The county judge is more involved in coordination than in control. It should be emphasized that the county judge is not a chief executive with broad policymaking authority. He or she does not control the budget, appoint department heads, or initiate major policies.

Other Elected Officials

The sheriff serves as the chief law-enforcement officer in the county, and in counties of less than ten thousand, the sheriff also serves as tax assessor and collector. Other elected officials include the justice of the peace (who has jurisdiction over some misdemeanors and civil issues within the precinct and may serve as county coroner in smaller counties), the constable, the county clerk, the assessor and collector of taxes, the treasurer, and the county attorney.

The Problems with County Government

Executive authority in county government is fragmented, and there is no chief executive with the power to implement policies or enforce compliance. There is essentially no centralized supervision of personnel or finances, and departments are free to choose their own course of action. Yet to change the authority and structure of county government would require changes in the constitution and state law. This would be very difficult to achieve due to tradition, apathy, and entrenched interests. When the state constitution was written, Texas was a rural state. Government was small, its scope and responsibilities were extremely limited, and public services and programs were provided at a minimal level. Consequently, county governments, with their weak powers, limited role, and minimal programs, were well suited to the needs of the time. Today, however, Texas is a heavily urbanized state with a complex economy, a huge and diverse population, and a variety of significant problems. County government is simply unequipped by virtue of authority or tradition to deal with these needs and problems.

Property taxes are the single-largest source of revenue for urban counties. Federal aid is not very significant when compared to property tax revenues. Since county governments receive relatively little help from federal and state government, they are heavily dependent upon local taxes. Because a single county may have an array of budgets (often as many as ten), it is very difficult to determine exactly how county funds are allocated. Counties also tend to lump together money spent on different services into one category, making the determination of allocation even more difficult. Although road and bridge maintenance is a primary responsibility of the county government, it is not the greatest expenditure for many large counties in Texas. Law enforcement and administrative expenses tend to be the greatest expenditure in urban counties. Social welfare, educational, and recreational services receive little attention in most county budgets. County government in Texas is primarily concerned with law enforcement and roads.

Special Districts

Special districts are considered the "hidden" governments of the state, many of which are water districts. Water districts in Texas include municipal utility districts (MUDs), water control and improvement districts (WCIDs), drainage districts, navigation districts, and river authorities. Water districts perform several functions. The state constitution gives MUDs the authority to provide water and hydroelectric power, to conserve natural resources, to combat water pollution, to provide park and recreational facilities, to dispose of sewage, and to collect solid waste. WCIDs may have all the powers of MUDs with the exception of the authority to provide park and recreation facilities. Other WCIDs, established under a specific legislative article, can undertake flood control, irrigation, navigation, and drainage programs. As can be seen in Table 12.2, other types of special districts include housing and redevelopment authorities, soil conservation districts, and hospital districts. Reliance on special-district governments has greatly increased in the past forty years. In 1950, there were only 490 in the entire state. That number had increased to 1200 in 1970, 1650 in 1980, and 1892 in 1987.

The increase in number of special districts can be attributed to several factors, including:

- Inability of existing governments to deal with problems
- Unwillingness of existing governments to deal with problems
- Unwillingness of existing governments to cooperate in dealing with areawide problems
- Taxing and debt ceilings that encourage the creation of new governments when these constraints prohibit existing governments from undertaking new services.

Special districts are easy to create and are usually established to deal with particular service problems. These districts may also be created by residential builders and developers who use the services of the district and then shift the cost burden to those who eventually buy the homes. Special districts may also be created to obtain federal aid.

TABLE 12.2 Special Districts by Function

Function	Number of Special Districts
Airports	3
Drainage and Flood Control	112
Fire Protection	70
Hospitals and Health Care	141
Housing and Community Development	396
Irrigation	73
Natural Resources and Water Supply	16
Parks and Recreation	3
Sewerage and Related Water Service	483
Soil and Water Conservation	210
Transportation (besides airports)	221
Utilities	139
Other	25
	1,892

Source: U.S. Bureau of the Census, *Census of Governments, 1987: Government Organization.* Washington, D.C., 1988, pp. 20–21.

Criticisms of special districts include the following:

- They are subject to little or no supervision by the state
- Their government is neither responsive or accountable
- They can compound local problems rather than solve them
- They add another layer of government to local areas that already have more than enough separate governments.

For all the criticisms, special districts are a result of local government's inability to deal with certain problems that they cannot or will not confront. Although their effectiveness is questionable, they are unlikely to diminish in number or significance in the near future. The widespread use of special districts reflects a fundamental attitude toward political power in the state. This attitude holds that public power should be limited. When government is absolutely necessary, it should be held to the bare necessities in terms of scope, responsibilities, and programs. In order to prevent government from adversely affecting the interests of powerful private groups in the state, political power should be divided up and fragmented among a variety of competing and separate governmental entities and jurisdictions. Instead of equipping existing governments with broad authority and resources to deal with areawide problems, new and weak governments should be created to deal with each new problem that arises. In that way, the consolidation of political power in the hands of existing governments—cities and counties—can be prevented. The intent is to limit public power and enhance the power of private interests. The proliferation of special-district governments represents the triumph of this philosophy.

Summary

1. Public education in Texas is controlled by more than a thousand school districts. Each district is governed by a school board elected by the voters in each district. The board hires the superintendent and teachers, sets the property tax rate, approves the budget, and establishes broad policy for the district.

2. In *Edgewood* v. *Kirby*, a state court held that variations in educational expenditures across school districts based on unequal access to property wealth were unconstitutional. In 1991, there existed a 585-to-1 disparity in property wealth between the richest and poorest school districts. The *Edgewood* decision will have a major impact upon the equalization of public education expenditures in the state.

3. The county is the major form of local government in rural areas and is assuming major responsibilities in urban areas as well. However, counties are ill suited to perform their duties. County government is simply unequipped by virtue of constitutional authority to deal with the needs and problems of a modern society.

---

4. Executive authority in county government is fragmented. There is no chief executive with the power to implement policies or enforce compliance. There is no centralized supervision of personnel or finances, and departments are free to choose their own course of action.

5. Special districts are the "hidden" governments of the state. They include water districts, drainage districts, river authorities, navigation districts, hospital districts, and housing and redevelopment authorities.

6. Special districts are subject to little or no supervision by the state. Special districts compound local problems rather than solve them. However, their popularity can be attributed to the inability or unwillingness to existing governments to deal with their problems.

References

Norwood, Robert E. 1970. *Texas County Government*. Austin: Texas Research League.

Pettus, Beryl P. 1974. "Metropolitan Area Multi-Purpose District Government in Texas," *Municipal Matrix* 6 (December 1974).

Tucker, Harvey. 1983. *An Assessment of Needs and Legislative Priorities of Texas Metropolitan Government*. College Station: Texas A&M University.

13

Regulatory Policy

Most Texans, like most Americans, probably assume that the federal government has the greatest power and responsibility for the regulation of private business. And Uncle Sam is indeed quite powerful in this respect. But state and local governments actually have greater responsibilities in terms of the variety of business and professional enterprises over which they have direct power *and* the breadth of their regulatory concerns.

Most Texans, and most Americans, also probably assume that it is only the regulation of business that concerns government. Most of us believe, that is, that government's only interest is in restricting business enterprise. We often think, as well, that the burden of regulation is too heavy and costly. Yet all levels of American government also have extensive policies intended to subsidize business. The goal of the latter policies is to ensure a healthy climate for business activity and even, in some instances, literally to maximize the profit-making opportunities for business. Thus both subsidy and regulation are carried out by Texas governments, and we cannot fully appreciate the work of these governments without understanding such activities.

State Government Responsibilities

State government agencies are responsible for a major share of these regulatory and subsidy activities, and the scope of their responsibilities is quite impressive. One or more state agencies exists, first, to regulate and sometimes subsidize a wide variety of the state's industries, including the following: agriculture (the Texas Department of Agriculture), alcoholic beverage sales (the Alcoholic Beverage Commission), banking (the Banking Department, the State Finance Commission, and the Savings and Loan Department), credit unions (the Credit Union Department), health care (the Department of Health and the Department of Human Services, among several others), insurance (the State Board of Insurance), natural gas and electric utilities (the Public Utilities Commission), nursing homes (the Board of Licensure for Nursing Home Administrators, along with several others), crude oil and natural gas production (the Railroad Commission), railroads (the Railroad Commission), and real estate (the Real Estate Commission).

In addition, various state agencies regulate such general business matters as employment practices, fair trade practices, labor relations, securities and stock issuances, occupational safety, air and water pollution, general waste disposal, and the use and disposal of hazardous substances. (Neither of the preceding lists is fully comprehensive, by the way, because the state has so many regulatory and subsidy responsibilities.) Finally, state agencies regulate a host of specific occupations and professions, as we will explain in more detail.

Most Texans understand the general principles of regulation, whether they believe it is a good thing or not. The government restricts the activities of business to help ensure such goals as fair competition, fair treatment of consumers, public safety and health, and the preservation of natural resources and the environment. How much regulatory responsibility government should have and how successful it is with its regulatory efforts are, of course, controversial subjects.

But what about the subsidy responsibilities of state and local government? We suspect that the average Texan is less well informed about such activities. Yet a host of state agencies subsidizes private businesses by such means as providing services, information, relief from regulation, or tax breaks; granting monopoly power to selected firms or individuals; or otherwise limiting the extent of competition in the industry to ensure a particular level of profit to those engaged in it.

For some specific examples of such subsidy, consider the work of the Texas Department of Commerce, an agency created in 1987 to promote the economic development of the state. The department has summarized its principal goals as "attracting national and international industries to Texas; promoting tourism in the state; and retaining and expanding businesses in Texas." All Texans may benefit to the extent that the department is successful in the pursuit of these goals, but individual business firms get direct and immediate subsidies as a product of the department's work. Consider just a few examples of the many subsidies offered by this agency and its various programs and offices, also as summarized by the department:

> "The Rural Industrial Loan Fund is available to manufacturing and industrial businesses in rural areas."

> "Export financial assistance is provided to businesses exporting products from Texas."

> "Financial assistance is provided to Texas businesses . . . for development and expansion."

> "The Enterprise Zone Program provides investment incentives, tax benefits, and regulatory relief to businesses in economically distressed areas of Texas."

> "Texas businesses preparing to expand can receive financial analysis and recommendations on appropriate public sector funding."

> "The Office of Small Business Development provides general business counselling and information to new and established small businesses."

This department, we repeat, is but one of a number of agencies with subsidy functions. We suspect that the extent of business subsidy that the state should provide, the success of its efforts of this kind, and the degree to which average Texans—as opposed to the subsidized businesses—benefit from those efforts would also be controversial questions for well-informed Texans. We offer no position on those questions ourselves, but we invite our readers to consider the pros and cons of business subsidy just as they do those of business regulation. Doubtless, both of these activities are appropriate for government. Both should also be carried out in a manner that balances the general health of business with other concerns, such as the fair treatment of consumers, public health and safety, and so on. We also suspect, however, that different Texans will take widely different positions on exactly how that balance of concerns will be settled with any particular regulatory effort.

Local Government Responsibilities

Local governments, and cities in particular, also have a variety of regulatory and subsidy functions. A good place to find a catalogue of such activities is in the city code of a home-rule city. Recall from Chapter 10 that the city code is the collection of laws made by a home-rule city itself for enforcing within its borders. The table on page 121 lists some businesses and business activities commonly regulated by Texas cities. Doubtless, this list ranges from the mundane—such as the regulation of dance halls—to the magnificent—such as the regulation of air pollution, buildings, transportation, and waste disposal. It indicates well, however, the broad range of local government regulatory responsibilities. And we urge the reader to remember that these regulatory functions are but a small part of all the things local governments do.

The Regulation of Professions and Occupations

State and local governments also regulate a considerable number of professions and occupations, as noted previously. The greatest number of these are regulated by the state, and the table on page 122 lists just those professions and occupations that are regulated by their own specialized state agency. (A good many other professions and occupations are regulated, licensed, or certified by other broad purpose or policy area-specific state agencies.) Doubtless, physicians, lawyers, police officers, and teachers would be counted among the most consequential of

Businesses and Activities Commonly Regulated by Texas Cities

Adult arcades
Air pollution
Alcoholic beverages
Amusements including carnivals, dance halls, golf courses,
   driving ranges, and archery ranges
Animals and fowl
Antique dealers
Automobile dealers
Automobile wreckers
Aviation, including airports, heliports, aircraft, and airport
   ground transportation
Building codes and standards
Burglar and fire alarm protective services
Food establishments
Flood hazard areas
Housing discrimination
Itinerant vendors
Massage establishments
Mini-warehouses
Mobile homes and mobile home parks and sales lots
Oil and gas wells
Railroads
Rat control
Residential subdivision plans
School vehicles
Sexually oriented businesses
Sight-seeing, charter, and limousine services
Swimming pools
Taxis
Tire storage and tire centers
Transportation of hazardous wastes
Vending machines

Professions with Separate State Regulatory Agencies

Accountants
Architects
Athletic trainers
Attorneys
Barbers
Chiropractors
Cosmetologists
Counselors
Court reporters
Dentists
Dietitians
Engineers
Fire fighters
Hearing-aid fitters
Law-enforcement officers
Morticians
Nurses
Nursing-home administrators
Occupational therapists
Optometrists
Pest-control workers
Pharmacists
Physical therapists
Physicians
Plumbers
Podiatrists
Polygraph operators
Private investigators
Psychologists
Real estate agents and brokers
Speech pathologists
Surveyors
Tax professionals
Teachers
Veterinarians
Water-well drillers

these regulated professions, while cosmetologists and hearing aid fitters, among others, might generally be considered less important. Regardless of how we react to any of the individual occupations included in the list, however, the table surely indicates the broad scope of such regulation. And considering that such regulation includes professions as wide-ranging as physicians and morticians, we can fairly say the state has "cradle-to-grave" responsibilities for all its citizens through these activities.

Why regulate the professions? In part, the answer is the same one given earlier for all business regulation—to protect the general public from unscrupulous and incompetent practitioners. But another motive has been widely noted as well. Regulation restricts entry into the profession. The number of practitioners is limited, the ways in which they practice are limited, and the potential profits for those in the profession are thus enhanced. This argument is buttressed by the fact that most state regulation of the professions is actually self-regulation. The state allows those already in the profession to establish the criteria for admission and the standards for practice. Then the state grants its power to those individuals to enforce these criteria and standards as law. Members of the regulated profession typically run the state agency that carries out the actual regulation. In effect, this argument suggests that state power is used to subsidize those in the profession by ensuring that they will collectively have a monopoly over the provision of certain services and goods to the public.

Consumer-Interest Regulation

Every Texan is a consumer. At a minimum we buy food, clothing, and shelter, and most of us buy a good deal more in the way of consumer goods and of professional and personal services and products. State government, in particular, has promulgated a variety of laws to assist the consumer. One motivation for the regulation of the professions, as noted above, is the protection of those who use their services. The regulation of most of the other industries and business practices discussed earlier in this chapter is motivated in part, as well, by a concern for the interests of consumers.

One additional, prominent means for protecting the rights of consumers is through the state's Deceptive Trade Practices-Consumer Protection Act, passed in 1973. This statutory law outlaws "false, misleading, or deceptive acts or practices in the conduct of any trade or commerce," and it provides for a variety of remedies and damages to those harmed by such acts or practices. Any Texan who believes he or she has been victimized by a deceptive business practice should call the Consumer Protection Division of the Texas attorney general's office for advice on how to pursue legal action.

Besides the broad protection provided by the trade practices law, other state laws target particular rights of consumers. Various state and federal laws regulate the warranties that manufacturers provide with consumer products. The Texas Debt Collection Practices Act limits the ways debt collectors can seek payment of outstanding debts. State law also ensures various rights of tenants—and for that matter, of their landlords—especially with regard to lease agreements, security deposits, landlords' claims for damages to be paid out of the security deposit, and landlords' obligations for repairs that ensure the property will be a fit place to live. Another notable piece of consumer legislation is the state's "lemon law," which aids individuals who purchase chronically defective automobiles. The accompanying box explains how to make a complaint under the provisions of the "lemon law."

FILING A COMPLAINT

Under the Texas *"lemon law"* buyers of new cars or other road vehicles may take their case to the Texas Motor Vehicle Commission.

1. If you choose to seek help from the commission, you should **file your complaint no later than six months after expiration of the first year of ownership,** or six months after the warranty has expired, whichever is earlier. The sooner you file your complaint, the better.

2. The commission will first attempt to resolve your problem on an informal basis. If no resolution is reached, the commission will hold a hearing at or near the consumer's hometown. **The commission does not require participants to be represented by attorneys.** Most consumers represent themselves, but you may have a lawyer or other advisor present if you wish.

While you don't need a lawyer for the hearing, you may bring one if you like.

3. Your chances of getting a refund or replacement are best under the following circumstances:

- If your vehicle has been out of your hands for repairs for **a month or more** during the warranty period, OR you have had the same defect repaired **four or more times and it still exists.**
- If the defect is a substantial one, especially involving parts which are expected to last for many years.

Remember: your complaint must be about an actual defect covered by the warranty, not simply a feature of the vehicle which you dislike.

<table>
<tr>
<td style="vertical-align:top; width:30%;">

You can file a complaint even after using the manufacturer's arbitration program.

</td>
<td style="vertical-align:top;">

4. The commission has authority to order a refund or replacement of any defective vehicle purchased on or after October 1, 1983. Other rules apply to vehicles purchased before that date.

If you have any questions about your rights as a new car owner, you may contact the commission in Austin at 512/476-3587.

ARBITRATION

Several manufacturers have set up their own arbitration programs. These programs usually involve a consumer arbitration board, which tries to resolve the problems consumers have with either the manufacturer or the dealer. If you decide to use this arbitration program first and don't get the problem resolved, you can still file a complaint with the Texas Motor Vehicle Commission later.

</td>
</tr>
</table>

Source: Texas Attorney General's Office.

Summary

1. Texas state and local governments have numerous laws and policies to regulate and to subsidize business.

2. State and local governments also regulate and subsidize a large number of professions and occupations.

3. A host of government agencies has been created to carry out these policy activities.

4. One major goal of business subsidy is to enhance the profits of the business sector and, presumably, to ensure the general economic health of the state for all Texans.

5. One major goal of business regulation is to protect the rights of consumers. A number of laws, like the "lemon law," provide direct means for Texans to appeal to government to ensure these rights.

14

Social Services

State and local governments dispense a wide range of social services to individual Texans. In fact, a major function of all governments in America today is providing such services. The most important of these services provide educational, healthcare, or welfare benefits. And these are, indeed, prominent responsibilities of Texas governments. As testimony to that fact, educational, health, and welfare programs account for about 67 percent of the state government's annual budget.

One can fairly think of these social services as *subsidies* much like those discussed in Chapter 13 that are provided to business. In this case, however, the government subsidizes individuals by giving them either services or money to buy goods and services that they otherwise could not afford. Just as in the case of business subsidies, social services are controversial. Some people believe government provides too many; others believe too few are provided. Surely our readers have a wide variety of opinions on that matter, too, but our goal in this chapter is not to make a case for any particular opinion about government's social service role. What we will do is offer some facts about the services our governments provide to help readers reach better-informed opinions. In addition, the chapter may acquaint readers with information about services they wish to get from government.

Undergraduate College and University Education

A very useful example of a social service subsidy is an education provided by a state college or university. Most people, and most college students, may not think of college education as a subsidy, but it is precisely that. It is true that college students pay tuition and other fees as a requirement for receiving this service from a state college or university. Many of those students also believe that college educations are not cheap, either. A common automobile bumper sticker in Texas says "My son (or daughter) and my money go to ___________ University." But a lot of other Texans' money also goes to those colleges and universities to subsidize the cost of each student's education.

In general, student tuition and fees amount to less than 25 percent of the revenues of colleges and universities. The bulk of the remaining revenue is provided by other taxpayers. Those taxpayers generously subsidize college costs with the hope that having better-educated workers, voters, and citizens will provide numerous benefits to us all. But individual, college-educated Texans will reap enormous personal benefits, too. A college degree is worth many thousands of dollars in future income that a person without a degree is very unlikely to earn. Thus here is one notable government subsidy of individual Texans. Is it a worthy one? At what cost to the taxpayers instead of to the students who will reap the individual benefits?

Health and Welfare Programs

The State of Texas also provides a host of health and welfare services and benefits. Some of these benefits are paid for by the U.S. government, while state and local governments actually operate the programs that deliver the benefits. In other cases the state both foots the bill and operates the program. Regardless of where the money originates, the expectation for all these programs is much the same as that for providing higher education. We hope that by providing for the health and welfare of the needy all of us will derive benefits. We might ensure by this effort that we have a healthier and more vigorous workforce. We might reduce the level of crime. And some would say we simply carry out an obligation of humanity to our fellow men and women who are in need. Doubtless, too, the recipients of these services reap individual benefits, just like the college students. They gain a good or service, the cost of which is borne by other taxpayers.

There are so many different programs and services in this broad category that we cannot discuss them individually. The accompanying box, however, lists the major state government agencies that provide such benefits, and summarizes their principal activities. The information indicates the breadth of these social services. Because the cost for these services is shared by federal, state, and local governments, it is difficult to estimate the total cost for any one program alone, as we did with educational programs. Thus we cannot compare the cost of a program to the likely benefits gained by the individual recipient as opposed to the taxpayers of the state at large. But the same question we asked about other social services is relevant here. Are these subsidies worthwhile? At what cost to the taxpayers to provide what level of benefits to the recipients?

The Generosity of Social Services

Our discussion to this point could leave the impression that the taxpayers of this state pay a heavy tax burden for an extensive array of social services. It is true that there are many social service agencies and that they provide a wide range of services. It is also true that the state spends a large percentage of its budget on education, health, and welfare. Some of that educational spending, however, is on elementary and secondary education, which many people would believe is justifiable when other social services are not. Similarly, subsidizing college educations would be readily accepted by some people who would not want to subsidize many health or welfare benefits. Thus whether our state's social service effort is large or small depends in part on what one is willing to call a social subsidy. And different Texans will have different opinions on that matter.

The size of the social-service effort is also a product of how

---

Health and Welfare Agencies and Benefits

Department on Aging

Since 1965, the Department on Aging has served as the state agency responsible for administration of the federal Older Americans Act. Originally created as the Governor's Committee on Aging, the agency was restructured by the Legislature in 1981 and given its current name. The functions of the department include planning and coordination of services, development and demonstration of programs, operation of an ombudsman program for persons receiving long-term care, provision of technical assistance to public and private service providers, and administration of grants to local service contractors.

Direct services for elderly clients are provided primarily through a network of twenty-eight local Area Agencies on Aging, which are usually affiliated with local Councils of Government.

Commission on Alcohol and Drug Abuse

The Texas Commission on Alcohol and Drug Abuse (TCADA) was originally created in 1953 as the Texas Commission on Alcoholism. The agency was given the added responsibility of administering the state drug abuse program in 1986, thereby enhancing the state's ability to address chemical dependency problems.

TCADA's primary mission is to coordinate alcohol and drug abuse services of state and local agencies through the development of education and prevention programs. The commission also seeks to protect the consumer and the public through licensure of alcohol and drug abuse treatment programs, certification of Driving While Intoxicated (DWI) education programs, and investigation of charges on client abuse, neglect, or other violations of client rights.

Commission for the Blind

The Commission for the Blind provides an array of services to blind and visually impaired children and adults. These services are designed to prevent vision loss when possible, and to assist the visually impaired individual in leading an independent and productive life.

REHABILITATION SERVICES
Rehabilitation Services are directed toward the following objec-

tives to prevent blindness and restore vision whenever possible, to provide supportive services that minimize the disabling consequences of serious visual loss when restoration is not possible, and to assist visually handicapped adults in obtaining and/or maintaining employment.

OTHER SERVICES

The Blind and Visually Impaired Children's Program has two basic objectives. First, through early detection and intervention, this program attempts to prevent blindness and to conserve eyesight. Second, when the prevention or correction of a serious visual impairment is medically impossible, caseworkers assigned to this program work with the child, the child's family, local schools, and appropriate community organizations to assist the child in overcoming the problems associated with serious sight loss. Some of the services provided or arranged include: eye restoration to prevent blindness or restore vision, adaptive aids and appliances, educational support services, counseling and guidance for clients and parents, and diagnostics and evaluations.

The Older Blind Services/Independent Living Rehabilitation Program enables older blind Texans, and other profoundly disabled blind individuals who are not eligible for vocational rehabilitation services, to have access to such services as vision restoration and adaptive training to enable them to live independently in their home and community, thus eliminating or reducing the need for custodial or nursing care.

Commission for the Deaf

The Commission for the Deaf was created in 1971 to serve the deaf and the hearing impaired. The commission contracts with twenty-three community-based nonprofit councils for the deaf to provide the following activities: interpreter services, information and referral, services to the elderly deaf, and message relay. The agency also has interagency contracts for interpreting services with other state agencies and provides these services through its council network.

The commission is responsible for the Board for Evaluation of Interpreters, which conducts evaluations of interpreters and makes recommendations for certification of interpreters to the commission. The commission is mandated to maintain and make available to courts and to all interested entities a listing of legally certified interpreters and other certified interpreters.

The commission also conducts other programs, including: a telecommunication device for the deaf (TDD) loan/placement program for state agencies and emergency response centers, a safety communication sticker program for vehicles of drivers who are deaf, and a one-week outdoor training program for young persons who are deaf.

Texas Employment Commission

The Texas Employment Commission (TEC) was created by the Legislature in 1936 as the Texas Unemployment Compensation Commission. It was renamed in 1947 to indicate more clearly its function as both an employment service and an agency for the payment of unemployment benefits.

The responsibilities of the Employment Commission include:
- The operation of efficient employment service programs which will help individuals find employment and furnish employers with employees and personnel services.
- The operation of an unemployment insurance program that will assist the justifiably unemployed and cushion a community's economy from the detrimental effects of extensive unemployment.
- The development of labor market information that will aid in the assessment of employment and training problems and will promote overall economic development.

Department of Health

The Department of Health is the primary state agency established to deliver public health services. Public health services are involved in prevention of disease, prolonging of life, and promotion of physical health through organized community efforts. Typical activities include the control of community infections, education of the individual in principles of personal hygiene, organization of medical and nursing services, and the sanitation of the environment through organized community programs.

Program emphasis has shifted throughout the 110-year history of the department in accordance with the public health needs of the citizens of Texas. Current program emphasis is directed at the delivery of personal health services, preventable disease control, and environmental and consumer health protection.

Commission on Human Rights

The Commission on Human Rights was created in 1983. The purpose of the commission is to provide for the enforcement of the policies embodied in Title VII of the federal Civil Rights Act of 1964, the Age Discrimination and Employment Act of 1967, and the Rehabilitation Act of 1973. The commission has the authority to investigate and resolve complaints of employment discrimination based on race, color, national origin, religion, sex, age or handicapped status by private employers with at least fifteen employees and by all public employers, as well as by colleges and universities, employment agencies, and labor organizations. The commission also provides technical assistance to state agencies and to private employers in order to promote compliance with state and federal employment discrimination laws.

Department of Human Services

The Department of Human Services (DHS) is the largest of the Health and Human Services agencies, when ranked by total appropriations, and receives the second-largest appropriations of all state agencies. For the 1990–1991 biennium, appropriations to the department total $8,293.4 million, of which $3,066.2 million, or 37 percent, are general revenue-related funds. Federal funds received either on a grant basis or as matching funds for specific state expenditures provide the majority of the department's funding.

Most services of the department are provided to persons with incomes considerably lower than the federal poverty guidelines. Services targeted to low-income clients include income assistance, health care, family self-support services (such as child day care, employment services, and family planning), nursing home services, and community care for aged and disabled persons. Other programs of the department provide services to Texans regardless of income. These services include protective services for children and elderly and disabled persons, child care licensure, and disaster assistance.

Department of Mental Health and Mental Retardation

The Texas Department of Mental Health and Mental Retardation (TDMHMR) provides residential, treatment, and habilitative and support services to people with mental illness or mental retardation. The agency operates thirteen state schools for people with mental retardation, eight state hospitals and an adolescent residential treatment facility for people with mental illness, and five state centers that provide both mental health and mental retardation services. The network also includes thirty-five locally governed community MHMR centers with which the department contracts to provide residential and nonresidential services in every region of the state.

Texas Rehabilitation Commission

The Texas Rehabilitation Commission (TRC) is designated as the state's principal authority on the rehabilitation of disabled persons, except persons with visual impairments and the legally blind. The commission provides a broad array of services to its clientele through seven major programs: vocational rehabilitation, disability determination, extended rehabilitation, independent living, comprehensive medical rehabilitation, interagency transitional services, and supported employment. In addition, TRC provides administrative support services to the Governor's Committee for Disabled Persons, the Texas Planning Council for Development Disabilities, and the Texas Advisory Board of Occupational Therapy.

Veterans Commission

The state's responsibility for rendering assistance and counseling to all Texas veterans, their dependents, and survivors in matters pertaining to veterans' benefits and entitlements is vested in the Texas Veterans Commission.

The Department of Veterans Affairs, a federal agency formerly entitled Veterans Administration, carries out the laws enacted by the Congress of the United States for the benefit of veterans. Veterans' benefits are not granted automatically; therefore, the Veterans Commission, in conjunction with Veterans County Service Officers, assists veterans or their beneficiaries with the development and completion of equitable claims.

Source: Legislative Budget Board, *Fiscal Size Up, 1990–1991*. Austin, 1990.

generous the state is to the recipients of its services. We may subsidize the education of college students, but do we give them a "first-class" education comparable to that of the nation's best colleges? Or do we, instead, provide them a relatively inferior education? We may provide health and welfare to the needy, but how generous is that welfare?

If public spending on college students is a fair indicator of the quality of the education they receive, then Texas is not providing a first-class education. In 1989–1990, for example, Texas state government appropriations for higher education were estimated to be $4,341 per college student. The national average per-student appropriation across all the fifty states was $4,388 (Sharp, 1991:64). Thus Texas is providing only an average quality university education to its residents.

Comparable comparisons with other states indicate that Texas is even less generous in its welfare effort, as we observed in Chapter 2. During the debate in the Texas legislature in 1991 about how to solve the state's budgetary woes, one lawmaker reported that Texas ranked forty-eighth among the fifty states in spending for welfare, forty-eighth for public-health spending, forty-seventh for Aid to Families with Dependent Children benefits, forty-seventh in benefits to senior citizens, forty-sixth in unemployment benefits, forty-fourth in benefits for the retarded, thirty-eighth for mental health programs, and fiftieth in state spending to fight alcohol and drug abuse. And the lean budget the state legislature produced in 1991 meant that we will likely fall even lower in these nationwide rankings.

Compared to the other American states, then, Texas has a remarkably modest commitment to social services, and Texas taxpayers shoulder a remarkably light burden for such services. The recipients of these services doubtless get real assistance from the state, but the amount of that assistance is quite modest in comparison to that provided by virtually all other states.

Summary

1. Texas state and local governments provide a number of social services to residents of the state.

2. We typically only think of welfare to the needy as constitut-

ing social services. Yet many not-so-needy Texans, such as college students, get notable social services subsidized by the state as well.

3. Texas is not a generous provider of these services when it is compared to other states. College students, as one example, do not pay for a very large part of the cost of their education, but the total cost of their education is not very high, either. In effect, the state does not spend much to educate them and they are typically provided only an average-quality education. Similarly, the truly needy in Texas receive only very modest state services and benefits.

References

SHARP, JOHN. 1991. *Breaking the Mold: New Ways to Govern Texas.* Austin: Texas Comptroller of Public Accounts, volume 2, part I.